MATURING
INTO
YOURSELF

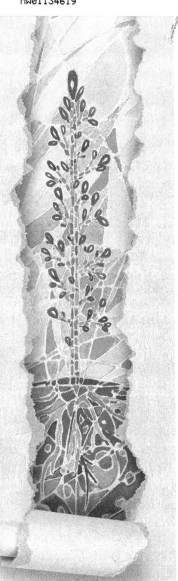

RAY LEIGHT

Maturing Into Yourself

Grow Into the Fullness of Your Healing

by Ray Leight

Table of Contents

DEDICATION

I would like to dedicate this book to all my friends and family who have believed in me, challenged me, loved me, and caused me to face my own wounds and pursue healing. You have each been a part of this journey and have helped make this book a possibility. Thank you!

ACKNOWLEDGEMENTS

I would like to acknowledge all my coaching clients who chose to pursue healing. It was your hunger, your questions, your desire for more of the kingdom and a life of freedom that motivated me to take on this project. Your dedication to being free and living in the truth of who you are is inspiring! Your feedback, testimonies, gratitude, and encouragement has been life changing for me. Thank you!

NOTE FROM THE AUTHOR

Welcome to the *Maturing into Yourself* process. This resource is an expression of many years of pursuing a healthy lifestyle and helping people understand the dynamics of what happens after a healing encounter. It started with the simple question of *"How do I walk this out?"* from many of my clients over the years.

This book is designed to help you grow into the fullness of your healing. I have put together what I have learned, as well as some wisdom from a few of the other coaches on our team. Heather Wright wrote chapter twenty-two, *Believing in Yourself.* Colleen De Silva wrote chapter twenty-three, *Dreaming Again.* Laura Burwick wrote chapter twenty-four, *Steps to Wholeness.*

GUEST AUTHOR

Heather Wright, Identity Coach

Chapter 22, Believing In Yourself

When I first met Jesus He gave me peace, love and joy like I had never experienced before in exchange for the mess my life was. He had me forever. This encounter led me on a quest to intimately know Him so I could share Him with others. I was surprised to discover that false beliefs and systems I unknowingly used to protect myself from pain were getting in the way of my desire being fulfilled.

As I've journeyed through healing, renewed thinking, and into new freedom I have found a closeness with Jesus, my Heavenly Father, and Holy Spirit. I have found a life lived from the inside out I never knew was possible—a life I'm passionate about, helping others find that this is available for everyone!

Heather has served in pastoral and teaching roles in several churches and independent ministries in the Mid-Valley area of Oregon, and as a pastoral counselor at the Bethel Transformation Center in Redding, CA where she trained under Ray and Kathryn Leight in Identity Coaching. She is currently an ordained minister with Global Fire Ministries International, based in Murfreesboro, TN. She's in love with her grandchildren, and is currently blessed with eight.

GUEST AUTHOR

Colleen De Silva, Dreams Coach

Chapter 23, Dreaming Again

Colleen De Silva discovered her joy to coach others in 2013. She has created tools to help her clients break free from the cycles that result from feeling lost and stuck. Colleen offers strategy sessions and dream interpretation as part of her coaching.

The strategy sessions help clients focus on their most rewarding daily tasks, so that they can conquer time management. Setting achievable goals allows Colleen's clients to walk in peace, be more present, and enjoy the process.

When Colleen interprets dreams, she partners with the Holy Spirit to discover practical and spiritual gifts, callings, and strategies. Many clients receive inner healing miracles and hope-filled perspectives that replace old habits and lies, moving them closer toward their dream life.

Colleen is also on her own dream-life journey. Today she lives in Los Angeles with her husband, Cory, where she pursues both her creative dreams and Dreams Coaching. She is an actress, writer, and entrepreneur. Colleen has a B.A. in English Literature from Indiana University, and is a graduate of Bethel's School of Supernatural Ministry in Redding, CA. Colleen loves pursuing the life that she loves and hopes to help others have the same discovery.

GUEST AUTHOR

Laura Burwick , Recovery Coach

Chapter 24, Practical Steps for Wholeness

Laura Burwick CADC II is a state certified drug and alcohol counselor, Sozo counselor, and an ordained pastor. She has been working with individuals and families for the past 30 plus years. She has worked in in-patient and out-patient treatment facilities, counseling centers and private practice. She is passionate about helping people identify their barriers so they can heal and have life more abundantly. Having worked in such a variety of settings Laura is well rounded and grounded in her approach to your emotional/spiritual healing journey. She provides counseling for individuals, families, couples and adolescences.

Laura has 3 children and 5 grandchildren. When asked why she loves being a counselor, she replied, "I have intentionally worked on building a legacy of healing and health for my own family. To have the opportunity to help others bring life and meaning into theirs is the greatest gift I could ask for."

He who descended is the one who also ascended far above all the heavens, that He might fill all things. And He gave the apostles, the prophets, the evangelists, the shepherds and teachers, to equip the saints for the work of ministry, for building up the body of Christ, until we all attain to the unity of the faith and of the knowledge of the Son of God, to mature manhood, to the measure of the stature of the fullness of Christ, so that we may no longer be children, tossed to and fro by the waves and carried about by every wind of doctrine, by human cunning, by craftiness in deceitful schemes. Rather, speaking the truth in love, we are to grow up in every way into Him who is the head, into Christ, from whom the whole body, joined and held together by every joint with which it is equipped, when each part is working properly, makes the body grow so that it builds itself up in love.

– Ephesians 4:10-16

CHAPTER ONE

Maturing Into Yourself

Welcome to your journey of maturity. This is a bold task not everyone is willing to take on. Congratulations for being courageous and open to pursue freedom and follow Jesus into life.

God loves you and created you in His image. He sacrificed Himself for you. He redeemed you with His own blood and reconciled you to Him. You are the joy that was set before Him, and the reason He endured the cross. He has delivered you from the dominion of darkness and transferred you to the kingdom of His beloved Son. This is who you are. You are redeemed, reconciled, delivered, loved, and forgiven. This is the life God wants for you.

Do you ever wonder why there are times when your behavior, your attitude, and your relationships don't express your Christ-like identity?

Healing is just a manifestation of truth.

If this is the case for you, don't be surprised. At some level, everyone is dealing with this issue. When you are experiencing this, it may be because you believe something other than what you know. I have found that everyone lives from what they believe, not what they know. That is why we have attitudes, actions, and behaviors that do not line up with the truth we "know." If you are reading this book, most likely you have had some type of healing experience and you are more aware of the disconnect between what you know, what you believe, and how you behave. This book will help you understand this issue so you can mature into yourself and walk out the truth of your identity in Christ.

Healing is just a manifestation of truth. The truth is already true. The work of the cross through Jesus' sacrifice is sufficient. We were healed by His wounds and restored to our righteous identity in Christ. If we are not experiencing the truth of who we are, it is because we do not believe that truth. Even though we have come to faith and have been born again as a new creation in Christ, we still hold on to some old lies and beliefs we have learned through our lives. These lies were established through many different methods of the enemy. We are all living in the false normal of the fallen world system. In this fallen world system, we will also have different cultural and generational lies that get passed down to us. Each one of us were born into a cultural and generational false normal. Regardless of how "Christian" our family was growing up, we grew up in a false normal that is not the kingdom of God. One of the problems with this is we usually do not have any understanding that something is wrong. It is just the way we experience, process, and see life. Sometimes we do not even realize we are not living in truth.

As we are growing up with these cultural and generational influences, we also experience traumatic events throughout our lives that cause us to believe lies. From the effects of these cultural, generational, and traumatic experiences, we then develop perspectives that cause us to see themes and patterns of lies that get affirmed in our beliefs. These belief systems are the root of the unhealthy self-protections of fear, shame, and guilt that we develop. I am not going to fully explain that process in this book. You can find the full explanation of this in my book *Identity Restoration*.

These self-generated systems of self-protection can be described in many ways. Some of the names for them are defense mechanisms, coping mechanisms, strongholds, ego, the imposter, or simply calling them reactions. I describe all of these as "systems of self-protections." At some degree, all of us are experiencing life this way. We sometimes react from a lie we believe, which was established in a previous situation, instead of being present and responding to what is happening in the moment.

Even though the truth of who we are is already true, we sometimes live out of lies we believe due to unresolved trauma. Remember, healing is just a manifestation of truth. To be more specific about the process of healing, I would describe it this way: Healing is a manifested revelation of truth, by faith, through spiritual discernment. When we believe the truth, we will live in that truth. We do not abide by knowledge; we abide by faith. In my opinion, it is impossible to mature into yourself without believing the truth of who you are.

We are whole in Christ, though we do not always live holistically in Christ. Somehow, beyond my ability to understand or explain, we compartmentalize. From this compartmentalization we react to these unhealthy belief systems instead of always being consistent. This is what commonly gets referred to as triggering. We will "trigger" into the emotional experience of an old unresolved trauma and react to different people and situations, differently, in fear, shame, and guilt because of the lie we believe associated with the past trauma.

What we are going to explore in this book are the different aspects of the maturing process. This process occurs when we have experienced revelation through spiritual discernment and now believe the truth of who we are. We are not going to walk through the healing process of repenting and believing in this book, so please refer to that process in my book *Identity Restoration* or schedule an Identity Coaching session at www.faithbygrace.org with one of our team members for more help.

In any maturing and growing process, there will be growing pains. In my opinion, the healing is the easy part. Jesus has already done all the hard work for us. Walking it out and allowing ourselves to be present, communicate our needs, and establish healthy boundaries is where the work is for us. This book will help you with all of this. We will be looking at what happens after we have repented from the compartmentalized lies we were believing, and now believe the truth. I hope this helps you walk out the truth of who you are.

CHAPTER TWO

Recalibration Process

There are many ways you can experience emotional and mental healing. You could have read the Scriptures, talked with a friend, had someone pray for you, experienced a vision, had a dream, listened to a teaching, read a book, had an inner healing session, gone to a counselor, had an Identity Coaching session, or prayed and asked God for healing. Regardless of the method, the source is always the same. Healing is a manifested revelation of truth, by faith, through spiritual discernment.

> The natural person does not accept the things of the Spirit of God, for they are folly to him, and he is not able to understand them because they are spiritually discerned.
> – 1 Corinthians 2:14

Healing is not an intellectual process; it is a spiritual process. The conviction and revelation of truth by the power of the Holy Spirit is what sets us free. Now that you have repented and believe the truth, you will experience the freedom that comes from truth. Remember, the truth of who you are is already true. We do not create truth by believing it. In these areas where you were previously experiencing fear, shame, or guilt, you were not believing the truth. You were believing lies. You were familiar with living life in the false normal you believed. This false normal began all the way back in the garden.

As soon as Adam and Eve believed the lie of the enemy, ate of the fruit, and began self-protecting, it changed their perspective, experiences, and expectations. This event transformed the kingdom reality that was intended for us into the false world system we now have. As time went on, people groups developed various cultural false normals that have impacted regions and societies differently. Then certain patterns and beliefs established themselves within family groups into generational false normals that have been handed down to us. Along with all this were the individual experiences and traumas that shaped our own personal false normals. All of these—the world, cultural, generational, and personal false normals—defined the reality we lived in. Now that you have encountered some healing from some of your false normals, you will experience life differently.

> When the Spirit of truth comes, He will guide you into all the truth, for He will not speak on His own authority, but whatever He hears He will speak, and He will declare to you the things that are to come. He will glorify Me, for He will take what is Mine and declare it to you. All that the Father has is Mine; therefore I said that He will take what is Mine and declare it to you.
> – John 16:13-15

In whatever way the Holy Spirit revealed truth to you, and you experienced healing, you will now have to become familiar with this new reality and mature into yourself. Usually, the first experience of this progression is the recalibration process. One or more of the compartmentalized areas of your heart where you believed a lie and were self-protecting has been redeemed. You now believe the truth, and your heart has been restored. You are experiencing freedom, peace, or joy in an area of your heart where you were experiencing fear, shame, or guilt.

Typically, this transition to freedom comes with a sense of disorientation, awkwardness, or weirdness. It is common for you to feel odd after you have experienced healing and freedom. The weird or odd feeling is not the freedom, it is the lack of familiarity to the freedom. This new feeling of freedom, peace, and joy is your new reality, it is just not familiar. You will eventually get used to this.

Many of the people I have worked with would describe this feeling to be like they just got off a boat or just got done skating. There is this oddness as you get used to walking on stable ground. The areas of your heart where you received healing were unstable. They are now stable, and you are in a process of becoming familiar with the stability. The recalibration process is like this boat and skating example, it is just more of an emotional and mental experience. Eventually, you will get used to the new reality, and freedom, peace, and joy will be normal in the areas of your heart that experienced healing. The weirdness will subside.

There is not something wrong if you are feeling off. The intensity of this feeling and the length of time you will experience it varies. It can even vary each time you experience healing. Sometimes it may last for weeks, sometimes hours or days. Just let yourself take the time you need to become familiar with your newfound freedom.

Your mind and your heart are in the process of recalibrating to this new reality. It is new, it is different, and it can sometimes be shocking. It can also be exciting and fun. There is a natural feeling of relief that you will experience along with this mental and emotional shift. The stress, pressure, and weight of the lies are not there anymore. As much as you can, take your time and be present in this feeling.

Your freedom is real, and you do not lose it just because it becomes familiar.

As you are enjoying the recalibration process, remember that the weirdness is not the freedom. It is the lack of familiarity to the freedom. As you begin to become familiar with your new reality the enemy will try to steal it from you. One of the common ways I have seen the enemy try to steal your newfound freedom is to tell you, "When the weird feeling goes away, the freedom goes away." That is not true. Your freedom is real, and you do not lose it just because it becomes familiar. You get to keep your freedom and live in it.

Another aspect of the recalibration and maturing process is the lack of understanding. We will not understand all the experiences we have. The recalibration process itself is almost a lack of understanding. It is OK that you do not understand the feelings you are experiencing right now. God's peace surpasses our understanding. If we attempt to understand everything, we may miss out on His peace.

> And the peace of God, which surpasses all understanding, will guard your hearts and your minds in Christ Jesus.
> – Philippians 4:7

There is so much more freedom ahead of you. This is going to be a fulfilling and exciting journey of discovering your identity, getting to know yourself better, and living out the truth of who you are. You have everything in you, in Christ, to be successful in your life. You can do this!

There are other nuances to the maturing into yourself process that we will continue to explore in the rest of this book. For now, celebrate whatever breakthrough you have experienced. Even if it was just a small step forward, celebrate your forward momentum!

CHAPTER THREE

Awareness

After a healing encounter, as you are going through the recalibration process, you will become more aware of what is happening around you and in you. This new awareness can be an interesting experience with challenges and opportunities of its own.

When you experience a situation that would have previously triggered you, you won't automatically trigger like you did before your healing. You will still have the same opportunities to trigger into an old traumatic experience, reconnect with a lie, and self-protect—but the healed areas of your heart will now respond differently. You will be more present and aware of the situation. When something seems wrong, you will be more connected with your thoughts and emotions in that situation. In the past when you would trigger, you were not fully present or aware of your emotions, thoughts, or reactions.

The circumstances of your life do not immediately change just because you are more free. The way you perceive these circumstances and the way you can respond in them will change. This is part of the awareness. You will become conscious of your new reality and you will notice that you do not automatically trigger into one of your self-protections and react the way you used to react.

As we previously looked at, these self-generated systems of self-protection can be described many ways. You may call them defense mechanisms, coping mechanisms, ego, strongholds, automatic reactions, or something entirely different. I describe all of these as "systems of self-protection." When I am talking about these systems, I am talking about how we automatically react in fear, shame, or guilt based on a lie we believe. Instead of being present mentally and emotionally in the moment, and responding to what is happening, we trigger into an old traumatic experience and react out of the lie associated with that trauma.

This new awareness will allow you to recognize the space, or the pause, that is happening in a situation where you now have a choice in how you can respond. This will be a new feeling in this area of your heart. You are not used to having space, or the ability to choose. You are familiar with automatically reacting in your protective system, and just accepting that as normal.

One of the challenges of this new awareness is that most likely you will not have the maturity to know how to handle the situation. You now get to be your true self in the situation and choose how to respond, you just do not have the years of experience of being yourself and choosing healthy responses. Being aware that something is off or wrong in a situation, does not necessarily mean you understand exactly what is happening and how to handle it. You will still need to grow in wisdom and discernment in these new areas of awareness.

Maturity is a process of emotional growth and personal responsibility for our own thoughts and feelings.

I have found that everywhere we believe a lie, compartmentalize, and self-protect, we stop emotionally maturing in that area of our heart. We may have become proficient at self-protecting because of a lie, but that is not maturity. At whatever emotional age we started protecting is where we will need to develop once we are healed. As adults, I realize immaturity is not something we like to admit. Maturity is a process of emotional growth and personal responsibility for our own thoughts and feelings. Time or intelligence are not the defining factors that influence it. Maturity is not based on your intellect or your age. The lack of experience you have of being personally responsible for your own thoughts and emotions, is the immaturity. Be OK with it and allow yourself to grow. At some level, all of us are in this process.

The good thing is, there are areas of your heart where you already believe the truth of who you are, have taken personal responsibility for your thoughts and feelings, and are mature. You can lean into this maturity, connect with God in the situation, and continue to grow into yourself. One of the tools I share with my Identity Coaching clients is the Three Steps to Life. These steps will help you to stay present, choose reality, connect with God, and be able to respond in a healthy way. If you want more information about these steps, as well as self-protections, they are fully explained in my book *Identity Restoration*.

For now, just know you will be more aware, but not always able to respond properly. You will make mistakes. It is OK. Do not expect yourself to handle everything perfectly because you now have experienced freedom. I still remember hearing stories early on in my mentoring and coaching ministry about people not responding properly in situations after experiencing healing. At that time, I did not know how to effectively communicate and help people through the maturing process. I was growing and learning myself. Some of the people that I worked with were using words like "freedom" and "healing," while acting very immature in their communities. This caused some issues with local pastors, and even caused some people to question the whole concept of inner healing.

Maturing into yourself can be a very messy process. It is not a simple, easy, serendipitous type of experience. You will have new emotions you need to process, new choices, new opportunities, new challenges, and new mistakes. You will need to learn how to appropriately express your needs and steward your emotions. You will need to practice and have patience for yourself.

One of the most common emotions people experience in this new awareness is frustration. You are now able to see what is happening, but you won't always know what to do about it or how to respond. This can be very frustrating. Do not confuse this with a lack of healing. This process reminds me of when young children become aware of, and try to do, an everyday practice we take for granted as adults. Similar to the frustration of a child learning to tie their own shoes, eat with a fork, or even walk down the stairs, you may find yourself wanting to throw a childish fit.

I have noticed with myself and many of my clients that along with the frustration and anger that can occur in the awareness process, there can also be a sense of discouragement or disappointment. In this new ability to be present in a situation, we will become more aware of our unhealthy relationships, patterns, behaviors, and mindsets. This can sometimes feel overwhelming and discouraging. It can almost feel worse than before and seem like we haven't even experienced any healing because we were not aware of how dysfunctional we were in the past. We will explore this more in the next two chapters. For now, just know that this type of response is sometimes part of the maturing process.

We will continue to look at the new choices you have, with your new awareness, in following chapters. It is OK, you can do this. It does get easier. If you allow yourself to stay present in your new awareness and take responsibility for your own thoughts and feelings, you will mature into yourself. The uncomfortable feelings you may be experiencing are worth it. I am continually amazed at the difference in my life. One day you will look back and be amazed at the change in your life as well.

CHAPTER FOUR

Old Tools

As we looked at in chapter three, one of the aspects of your new awareness will be the choices you have in a situation. With these choices comes a new responsibility. You can choose to stay present mentally and emotionally, communicate in a healthy way, and respond to the present situation out of the truth of who you are, or you can react in your old self-protection of fear, shame, or guilt. These new options of awareness and responsibility can sometimes be frustrating as you are trying to learn new habits and mature into yourself.

Part of the process of healing is being more aware of the old patterns and habits you have established over the years of self-protecting. Those habits and behavior patterns are still around. They do not magically disappear after a healing encounter. As you become more aware of these, it can seem like things are even worse than they were before. It may even trick you into thinking that you didn't have any

The awareness and the ability to choose are the evidence of healing.

healing at all. This is the opposite of the truth. The awareness and the ability to choose are the evidence of healing. In the past, you were somewhat unaware of your unhealthy reactions. You now have freedom and can mature into yourself as you stay present and learn how to make good choices.

Many of my Identity Coaching clients will discount this new awareness because of the frustration and discouragement that can accompany it. Don't discount this. This new awareness is a huge breakthrough! In the past you had no choice. You would automatically react in some form and maybe not even be aware of what was really happening. This new ability to be present in the situation, be aware that something isn't quite right, and discern an appropriate response is a dramatic improvement. Like I mentioned in the previous chapter, this process can be very messy. There is no need to be discouraged by this mess. It is part of the process of developing new healthy habits and behavior patterns.

Even though the area of your heart that was previously programmed to react in fear, shame, or guilt is redeemed, it doesn't mean you are now familiar with being free. You do not have the years of experience of being free, having peace, and being joyful in this area of your life. This is a new feeling, and you will need to develop new habits and mindsets. Freedom is always better; it just isn't always easy in the beginning.

One of the ways I describe these old habits and patterns of self-protection is to label them "old tools." You have years of training and experience using these old tools. Now, you have been upgraded and retooled. You just have no experience using these new tools. If you remember from the Awareness chapter, you not only have new tools to learn, but you are also emotionally immature in this area of your life. Think about it in terms of a job you may have. You have been trained and have years of experience using certain tools and programs. You could have even been using these same tools from the very beginning of your career. Now you have experienced a promotion and an upgrade. You have greater responsibilities, insight, and a better overview of the entire working operation. With this new position comes new tools and new programs you need to learn, all while you still must get the same job done. During this learning experience you also become aware of how dysfunctional the old tools and programs were. You can now see how disruptive the old systems were and you may become more sensitive to your surrounding environment and relationships. There could also be a sense of being overwhelmed and confused because of all the new information and the lack of needed emotional maturity. This can be a remarkably demanding time when you make mistakes and have to clean up messes. Don't worry, it's going to be OK. This is what it is like to experience healing.

Even though you may feel out of control, you are not. You were created and designed to handle this. God equipped you with everything you need to do what He has called you to do. In the past, you have not been expressing the true nature of your identity because of the lies you believed and the self-protections you were manifesting. Now you are able to be you. You will begin to naturally express your true nature of freedom, peace, and joy. You will also be able to use these new tools that God created for you.

This process of maturity will require you to intentionally stay present with yourself and your situation—mentally, emotionally, and physically. Let yourself be aware, able to breathe, able to think, and able to make good choices. The more you practice this new lifestyle of freedom, peace, and joy, the better you will get at living this way.

There will be times when you will be tempted to believe lies and self-protect. You will still pick up these old tools, out of habit and immaturity, and use them occasionally. But now it will be different. It won't feel as natural. Each time you try to use them you will be able to catch yourself, and you will catch it sooner and sooner. Have patience for yourself. Please remember, this is a common occurrence in the maturity process. The familiarity of these old tools will fade away. Eventually you may not even remember them. There is no reason to get discouraged or think you didn't experience healing if you catch yourself using these old tools. Remember, this awareness is a significant breakthrough!

The more you can take personal responsibility for your thoughts, emotions, and behaviors, the more you will mature.

It is OK if you catch yourself using the old tools. As much as possible, try to have grace and patience for yourself. Remember, it is a good thing that you can now understand you are using an unhealthy tool and can choose a healthy one. The more you can take personal responsibility for your thoughts, emotions, and behaviors, the more you will mature.

As you mature, you will begin to trust God and trust yourself in this area of your life. Trusting God, who created and healed you, and trusting yourself, is the evidence of healing. This trust will manifest itself in freedom, peace, and joy. You have what it takes, and you can do this.

CHAPTER FIVE

Functional Dysfunction

You may have noticed that the patterns in some of your relationships are no longer working for you. You are most likely becoming aware of your habits and behaviors that no longer seem to be acceptable. This type of revelation and understanding is part of the maturing process after a healing encounter.

Making the choice to pursue healing and to be free is no small task. Choosing to do the emotional work of discovering the lies, pain, habits, patterns, self-protections, and structures you have developed over the years because of your unresolved trauma, is a very courageous thing to do. Your honesty with yourself and with God in admitting you are not living in the fullness of His truth, is a sign of strength and character.

Your journey may be discounted, criticized, or challenged by others.

This is a common occurrence in an environment where people are trained to deny what is happening internally and to perform to the cultural expectations externally. Honesty, vulnerability, and the admission of any unbelief in our life is challenging in some social circles. Commonly and unfortunately, you may even experience this in your church. Don't let that worry you; you can do this!

Part of your journey of maturing into yourself will be the awareness of the dysfunctional relational patterns you have developed in your life. Unfortunately, we have all connected with and stayed in certain relationships and social groups due to the unhealthy systems we have in place. One of the reasons we will get into unhealthy relationships is because that type of interaction was already normal for us. The details of the relationship may be different, but the underlying patterns are the same. Sometimes, this can be a difficult and painful revelation.

> Everywhere that you were believing a lie and self-protecting in fear, shame, or guilt, there is a real need.

There are both healthy and unhealthy reasons we will engage in relationships. I describe this as "Functional Dysfunction." What I mean by this phenomenon is that we will be attracted to people for good, healthy reasons, and also for reasons that are not so good. The social patterns we experienced in our childhood will influence our relational choices and our acceptance of certain patterns that are not beneficial.

Everywhere that you were believing a lie and self-protecting in fear, shame, or guilt, there is a real need. Just because you were trying to get your needs met in an unhealthy way doesn't mean there wasn't a real need that needs to be met. Whatever unhealthy way you were trying to get your needs met before the healing encounter, is part of the dysfunctional pattern you will now start to notice. You still have the same real relational needs, you will just no longer automatically try to fulfill those needs in an unhealthy way. You will now begin to notice when someone tries to engage with you in those old unhealthy patterns. This is usually a very uncomfortable process.

Let me describe it in a practical way that may be easier to understand. I am going to use milk for the analogy. Imagine if you grew up drinking sour milk your whole life, thinking it was fresh, healthy milk. You became familiar with the flavor and made it a part of your regular diet. As you grew up, you established relationships with people who would provide you with sour milk. Each one of these relationships could vary in how much sour milk you received from them, and what you gave them in return. For example, maybe you would give them rotten fruit. You may even get to a place where there is an addiction to the milk, and you establish patterns and structures in your life to make sure you get it. You now have a regular delivery plan where you trade your rotten fruit for their sour milk. Then, you suddenly experience the taste of fresh, healthy milk. This healthy milk begins to transform your rotten fruit into healthy, fresh fruit. Your need and desire for the sour milk is no longer there like it was, and you now know the difference between sour and fresh milk. Now that you can discern and see the difference, don't have the need for the sour milk, and no longer have the rotten fruit available, it is going to disrupt some of your relationships. You will now be aware of the patterns you have established and the people you have been exchanging with. Those people are still going to deliver you the sour milk and expect to get the rotten fruit in return. In the past, you didn't really have a choice. You would habitually receive the sour milk and then automatically react in some preprogrammed manner with rotten fruit.

Now you have a choice. You do not need to receive the sour milk, and you do not automatically react. This would be the space, or pause, that I mentioned in the Awareness chapter.

Freedom is always better, and it does get easier.

Remember, even though you now know your real need and desire for healthy milk, you still have all these patterns and dysfunctional relationships in place. This is where you will need to mature into yourself. People may be rather upset that you will no longer accept their sour milk and may be frustrated that you no longer offer them the rotten fruit they want. Being able to analyze your relationships, communicate, establish boundaries, and develop new, healthy patterns can be difficult. This takes an intentionality to stay present, choose reality, and connect with God. We will look at that process in a future chapter. For now, just know that just like the milk analogy, you will no longer have the unhealthy need. You will have to go through the process of evaluating and restructuring relationships. Depending on the level of dysfunctional patterns in the relationships, you may even lose some of them. This can be a very tough process.

It can feel overwhelming as you become aware of the dysfunctional patterns and the unhealthy ways you have been trying to protect yourself and take care of your needs. You are still experiencing the unhealthy relationships you previously established. You can see it more clearly now, and you don't always know what to do. It is OK, you can do this. You will now be able to express the truth of who you are, and you will naturally grow into yourself. This can seem like a lot of work, but it is better than the old, unhealthy patterns. Freedom is always better, and it does get easier.

CHAPTER SIX

Pendulum Swing

During the maturing process, sometimes we will feel out of control and unable to stop an emotional or behavioral response. That can be an unhealthy pattern from an unresolved trauma, or it can be the pendulum swing that happens after a healing encounter.

As we examined, there are many behaviors, habits, and dysfunctional relational patterns we may have because of past trauma in our lives. In my own life, and with many of my coaching clients, I have seen a significant change in reactions after experiencing healing. Some of the changes are a healthy response out of the truth of who we are, and some of them are an immature response out of lack of experience. We are now free, but we are not mature in those areas of our heart. This immaturity and lack of experience can result in a response that is different from the usual, unhealthy reaction. Instead of reacting out of a wound, we may react out of immaturity. Often, these reactions will happen at the same level of intensity as the old, unhealthy pattern. This process can feel very unstable.

The instability that you may experience can be mistaken for a lack of healing. It can seem like you are behaving in the same type of unhealthy reaction you were before. This pendulum swing is not the same as the old, unhealthy reactions. The lack of experience of being able to just be yourself and respond healthily can sometimes cause you to react in a way that does not seem appropriate for the situation.

The truth of who we are is already true.

Being free does not mean you are mature. It is particularly important to understand that there is a maturity process. There are several places in God's Word where this is talked about. In Ephesians, the Scriptures tell us that He gave the apostles, prophets, evangelists, pastors, and teachers to equip the saints for the work of ministry. They help build up the body of Christ until we all attain the unity of the faith and of the knowledge of the Son of God. All of this is to bring us to maturity, being complete and perfect in the full measure of the stature of Christ. I am not sure about you, but I know my life does not always represent that! I personally have not met anyone who represents the full measure of maturity in Christ. We are all somewhere on this journey.

I believe that we are already whole in Christ, we just do not live holistically in Christ because of the lies we believe. Healing is just a manifested revelation of truth, by faith, through spiritual discernment. The truth of who we are is already true. As we begin to believe the truth, we will experience the truth, and we will mature into our true identity in Christ. This is a process that we need to allow ourselves permission and grace to go through.

When we now experience the same triggering circumstances, we do not have the same automatic reactions. We do still have all the years of unhealthy training, habits, behavioral patterns, relational issues, and dysfunction. We will need to learn how to be present, communicate our needs, establish new boundaries, and develop healthy relational patterns. The pendulum swing during this process can look different for each one of us. Consider the following example. Maybe someone had unhealthy codependent relationships in which they tried to please people and had trouble telling people no. After they experience healing in this area of their life and no longer have the unhealthy need to please people, they may have an extreme contrasting response of not wanting to do anything for people. Then they could potentially feel bad about that reaction and move back toward people pleasing again. After that, they may get frustrated by the people pleasing and then react in a negative way toward people who want anything from them. This back-and-forth process will often happen as they try to be present, figure out their real needs in the situation, learn how to communicate, and establish healthy boundaries.

If you picture a pendulum for a moment and think about the previous example, it may make more sense to you. When you know and believe the truth of who you are, there can be an established, balanced, central point from where you live your life. This would represent a pendulum that is not being pulled to one side or the other. But, if instead of being balanced, you have been stuck in an area of your life, pulling you in one direction that now has been released, the weight of that off-balanced aspect of your life will naturally swing back and forth until you find your healthy center. This can be an incredibly challenging experience as you are more aware of the dysfunctional patterns in your life and now have the personal responsibility of having choices.

During this process, it is important to allow yourself to stay present and be aware of the pendulum swings of immaturity. As we react immaturely in the opposing reaction, it is possible to believe new lies and establish different unhealthy self-protections. You may express feelings of anger or frustration in this time due to a feeling of powerlessness. Even though you can now see the dysfunction, you might not know how to respond. Though this can lead to feeling powerless, you must remember you are not! You now have the ability to make healthy choices and respond in a way that works for you.

Don't be afraid of the swings; they are not your identity.

There are people you are in relationship with who may not be happy with this "new you" who doesn't react in the way they are used to. These people may try to discourage your growth in an attempt to get you to conform to their desires. Being aware of your needs and your desires during this type of struggle is essential.

> I have said these things to you, that in Me you may have peace. In the world you will have tribulation. But take heart; I have overcome the world."
> – John 16:33

As much as you can, allow yourself to be present, be free, and enjoy your peace—you will be strengthened and mature into yourself. It is in this place of struggle, or tribulation, where the enemy is going to try to deceive you and trick you into believing new lies and developing new forms of self-protections. The world, the enemy, and sometimes the people you have dysfunctional relationships with do not want you free and healed. Don't be afraid of the swings; they are not your identity. You are a new creation, with a new clean heart, and you can live free.

It may take longer than you want, and it may be more work than you thought, but you can do this! You get to be you. You get to have needs, opinions, boundaries, and healthy relationships. Hold on, the swings become less extreme, and you get to have a balanced life. It is worth the extra effort now, as you will eventually enjoy the peace, joy, and freedom of who you are in Christ.

CHAPTER SEVEN

Letting Yourself Grieve

Once you can see an unhealthy situation or relationship clearly, you may experience a sense of loss. Sometimes, after a healing encounter, you may go through this type of grieving. This can be a very confusing process as you are trying to mature into yourself.

Part of the awareness that happens after we experience healing is that we will see a relationship or a situation for what it really is, not what we thought it was. We were unaware of many of the dysfunctional patterns that we lived in. The lies that have been established and self-protections we are using cause us to perceive things that are not reality. The Functional Dysfunction style relationships that we have had were normal for us. The self-protections we have created help us cope with abuse and trauma instead of confronting them and being able to establish healthy boundaries. These self-protections can become so familiar they almost become like a trusted friend.

As we engaged in these relationships through the lenses of our lies and self-protections, we could have perceived unhealthy behavior and abuse as being helpful, kind, or even loving. In some circumstances, it is shocking when we see what was really happening. It can even be hard to understand or accept what we are now aware of. This can add a whole new dynamic to the maturity process. I have seen hundreds of my coaching clients deal with this revelation.

You may experience a feeling of loss once you realize that you didn't have the relationship or situation you thought you had. Commonly, this need to grieve can be discouraging when it is confused with the misconception that there was no healing. It is important to remember that everyone's process is not the same. Even in your own maturing process, each healing experience can be different. Sometimes you may need to grieve, and other times you may not. There is no set pattern for how the healing and maturity process will affect each person. You are free to experience whatever you are feeling in your personal process.

To help you maybe understand this a little better, here is an excerpt from chapter thirteen, Abstract Loss, from my book *Finding A New Normal*:

Years ago, while working with some of my coaching clients, I noticed that after they received healing and freedom, they began to grieve. This was an interesting phenomenon that I did not understand at first. What I discovered is that people will see more clearly once they are set free from old, dysfunctional relational patterns. Once they can see the relationship for what it really is, they may need to grieve the loss of what they had perceived the relationship to be. This is an interesting set of circumstances that not everyone experiences, but many do. Having to let go of something you only "thought" you had, that you didn't really have, can be confusing and painful. Sometimes additional coaching was needed to help them get through the different dynamics of the relational shift. When this type of healing occurs, grieving is an important part of their healing process.

This was not the only abstract pattern of loss I noticed with my clients. I also found that sometimes when people received healing from more intricate and sophisticated self-protections, there would also be a need for grieving. Our systems of self-protection can become so familiar and comfortable that there can be a sense of loss after healing. It is almost like they became a trusted friend we had been relying on. There can even be an experience of loneliness as we recalibrate to our new life without this self-protection. If you need or want more information about how we use self-protections, my book *Identity Restoration* explains this topic.

I realize it is an odd concept that someone may need to grieve after receiving freedom and healing, but this is a real experience for some. Even in a good situation, like healing, there can be a need to let yourself grieve something you've lost. Remember, your loss doesn't have to be tangible in order to warrant the need for grieving.

I have found there can even be a need to grieve something that you only perceived you had. Our perceptions are our reality. When we lose something very meaningful to us, something we only perceived we had, it can be a real loss. Experiencing this significant reality shift can be very jarring to us emotionally and can initiate a need to recalibrate and adapt to a new normal. The grieving process allows us to adapt to this new normal.

The loss of what you thought you had, even though you did not really have it, is a real loss.

The loss of what you thought you had, even though you did not really have it, is a real loss. There can be a deep sadness that sets in after you are aware that the life and the relationships you thought you had were not reality. It is important to let yourself grieve through this loss.

There is not something wrong with you because you may be experiencing sadness and grief after a healing encounter. You get to be you! You are allowed to have your own thoughts, feelings, opinions, and needs. Recognizing your dysfunctional patterns, behaving immaturely, feeling the emotional swings, and grieving can be overwhelming. Don't get discouraged, you can do this. It does get easier, and you can live in freedom, peace, and joy.

CHAPTER EIGHT

Establishing Boundaries

To have healthy relationships, there needs to be intellectual, emotional, spiritual, and physical boundaries. I hear emotional and physical boundaries talked about quite often, with the most common being physical. I have not personally experienced intellectual boundaries being discussed often, even though I believe this is the most common boundary that is crossed in relationships.

Usually, but not every time, before there is a physical boundary crossed in a relationship, there has been a consistent pattern of emotional and intellectual boundary violations. If we are going to develop healthy relationships after a healing encounter, we will need to focus on honoring intellectual and emotional boundaries for ourselves and those we are in relationship with. This will allow us to also have healthy spiritual and physical boundaries with people.

If you do not know yourself, you cannot really know your needs.

There are many reasons why you may not have healthy relational boundaries. It could have been cultural or generational patterns, thematic abuse, one-time traumatic events, or simply a lack of training. All of these can keep you from truly knowing yourself. If you do not know yourself, you cannot really know your needs. With this lack of knowledge, along with unhealthy relational patterns, boundaries are not something that are really understood or communicated well. This is something I am still in the process of learning and maturing into myself. In some areas of my life, I still have problems communicating boundaries in a healthy way.

Now that you have experienced a healing encounter and have begun to recalibrate, you are most likely becoming more aware, having less extreme emotional swings, seeing the dysfunctional relational patterns in your life, and understanding your choices better. This is the maturing process. As you mature and get to know yourself better, you will need to give yourself permission to establish new, healthy boundaries.

Identity is so important in this process because all healthy boundaries develop from the truth of who you are. Without a solid foundation to establish them, boundaries will be difficult to implement and keep. Think about boundaries within the analogy of a home. Let's start with your yard. The initial set of boundaries would be represented by your fence. The fence itself will not be highly effective if there are not fence posts securing the fence line. The fence posts would represent the different aspects of your identity that you can securely connect to. If you are not secure in your identity, it would be like mounting your fence posts in mud or sand. These posts will float around or even fall over if pushed against because the ground is not solid. The posts need to be securely mounted so the fence can stay up and weather any storms. These storms could be analogous to the mental, emotional, or relational changes or traumas in your life. When you have your boundary posts established in solid ground, you can better weather these changes and traumas. Boundaries will also have a way in, just like a gate on a fence. You will be able to establish how that gate gets opened and who can enter.

Once someone is allowed in your yard, maybe you have a pool, a deck, and a shed with your lawn equipment and tools. Who is allowed in your yard, your pool, or on your deck? Who is allowed to come over and play in your yard, use your grill, or borrow your lawn equipment? Then there is the house itself. Who has keys to your house and can come in? Do you even lock your doors? Who is invited over and can have dinner with you, watch TV, or hang out in your basement? Then we even have more private areas in our home. Who is allowed in your bedroom, or your private bathroom? The respect you have for each of these different aspects of your home will determine the level of access and care of each.

Each one of these areas represented in this house analogy can abstractly be applied to our lives. There are different boundaries for different aspects of our life. Who has access to our thoughts and emotions? Who has access to us physically and spiritually? What level of access do they have to each of these? Now that you have experienced a healing, you will most likely see some unhealthy boundary issues and need to realign them.

When it comes to boundaries in your previously dysfunctional relationships, there is no way for me to know whether you were the boundary breaker or the one who did not have secure boundaries. You may be used to having boundaries yourself, but you were not honoring the boundaries of others. You could have allowed others to walk all over you without any healthy boundaries for yourself. More commonly it is a mixture of both. Regardless of how you previously experienced boundaries in relationships, it will be different now. The healing you experienced will allow you to better love yourself and love others. You will be able to honor your needs, and the needs of others, in a healthier way.

Allowing ourselves, and others, to have our own thoughts, our own feelings, believe our own beliefs, and have the right to exist and show up in our relationships is a life-giving and fulfilling experience. We were created for community. When we can allow ourselves and others to be and express our true selves, we will be able to build each other up, help each other, love each other, and take care of each other's needs in a healthy way. However, this may not always go well. Remember, you are trained in old, unhealthy tools and have not fully matured in your redeemed self yet. You will make mistakes, break boundaries, and engage in codependent patterns still. It is OK, you can learn from this and continue to mature.

Kingdom freedom does not violate other people's freedom.

A common issue with the maturing process is that people will challenge your new boundaries for several reasons. One is because they are just not used to them. Just like we looked at in the Functional Dysfunction chapter, you have all these behavioral patterns and habits that people are used to. Some relationships will need major overhauls, and some will need minor adjustments. This process can seem a little overwhelming and daunting if you overthink it. Let yourself be present, think your thoughts, feel your feelings, and process what you are experiencing in the moment. You do not have to fix everything right now. It will all work out. Just stay true to God, yourself, and your needs.

The truth of who you are naturally honors other people's boundaries and allows you to have your own. Kingdom freedom does not violate other people's freedom. The more you can believe and express the truth of who you are, the more you will honor and respect others. It is easier than you think to operate within healthy boundaries. As you become more comfortable with yourself and your needs, you will easily learn how to communicate and navigate relationships. We will continue to look at the different types of boundaries, how they are commonly broken, and how you can manage healthy relational boundaries in the following chapters.

You have everything you need to be able to do this. It may be uncomfortable at first, but believe me, the freedom, peace, and joy that is available in your relationships is worth the extra work now.

CHAPTER NINE

Intellectual Boundaries

Each one of us have our own thoughts and our own feelings. These thoughts and feelings exist in our internal world. We can share, communicate, empathize, relate, and express them—but they are our own. They do not belong to anyone else, and no one else's thoughts and feelings belong to us. This delineation is where it can get messy, blurred, painful, and confusing. In my opinion, the confusion around these boundaries is a big part of the reason why they are often violated.

Understanding the difference between thoughts and emotions is something many of my coaching clients need help processing. In chapter fourteen, I Think – I Feel, we will explore the boundaries between our own thoughts and feelings. I also explain the difference between thoughts and feelings and how they affect our perspectives in chapter five of my book *Identity Restoration*. In this book, we will be looking at boundaries around thoughts and feelings and how they are commonly violated.

Let's start with the idea of intellectual boundaries. What I mean by this is that we each have our own thoughts, intentions, motives, beliefs, and perspectives. All of these are unique to us. These have all been influenced through culture, our generational family traditions, our relationships, our experiences, and any traumatic events. We may have similar beliefs and thoughts, but no one has experienced exactly the same life as someone else and believes and thinks the same as them. What we believe and think about God, ourselves, and others will individually define how we experience our lives.

When I am talking about boundaries in these areas, what I am saying is that we do not have direct access to what other people have been through, what they are experiencing, what they are thinking, what their intentions are, what their motives are, what their beliefs are, or how they perceive the world around them. Other than what people will share and communicate with us, we only have access to our own.

These boundaries are violated when we define or think other people's thoughts for them. One of the most common issues my coaching clients need to process through is how they engage in thinking other people's thoughts for them. As you are processing your healing experience and maturing into yourself, you may be recovering from the damage of this process and how you perceived yourself because of it. Becoming aware of our thoughts and allowing other people to have their own thoughts separate from us is a significant part of the maturing process.

In several places in Scripture, Jesus knew other people's thoughts. It is possible for Holy Spirit to give you the knowledge of other people's thoughts. When Holy Spirit does this through spiritual discernment, it is different than the destructive patterns of thinking other people's thoughts for them or projecting our lies as other people's thoughts. I still remember what it was like before my first inner healing encounter. The lies I believed would cause me to read every situation and reaction from other people in a way that would confirm the lie I was already believing. What I thought was discernment was actually divination. This is a miserable practice that will cause fear, shame, and guilt. Discernment from Holy Spirit will not do that. A simple test to determine whether you are divining or discerning would be to see if the information comes with fear, shame, and guilt, or freedom, peace, and joy. So often, the clients I work with think they are discerning when they are just projecting their lies into other people's minds and seeing themselves through the lens of those lies. This is a violation of intellectual boundaries.

Reacting to how we think other people are thinking is one of the ways the enemy has deceived us into destroying our own relationships and community. It will keep us from being present, experiencing life, and having authentic relationships.

One of the common ways this happens is what my clients describe as "people pleasing." Think about that for a minute. Is that something you would consider to be an issue for yourself? Often people will engage in this process and say they are "trying to make sure that people are happy." In reality, I would consider this an intellectual boundary violation because what is really happening is that they are manipulating people and situations to try to get people to think a certain way about them. This is so much more of a problem than just intellectual boundary violations because it puts you in a continual loop of trying to manage your perception of people's thoughts about you with ongoing performances and behaviors. Not one of my clients has ever found this to fulfill the real need they have in the situation. Instead, it continues to confirm the lie they are believing that is causing them to perform and manipulate. I often see this behavioral loop disguised as "serving others." If you have received healing in this area of your life, you will most likely experience the pendulum swing that we looked at in chapter six. It is OK if you do; now that you can more clearly think your thoughts, you will be able to discover the things you want to do and don't want to do.

One of the other ways I see this played out in people's lives is that they will create an internal imaginary world they live in based on their perception of what other people think of them. Instead of being present in the moment and experiencing real life, they are reacting out of this imaginary world they have created and only get to observe other people living. This is so isolating and destructive. The experiences that some people have through their lives have influenced them to perceive other people's actions, behaviors, facial expressions, and words to mean certain things. So, instead of communicating properly and responding in the moment, they react out of the intentions, motives, thoughts, and beliefs they have predefined and assigned to these different interactions.

This behavior can lead to a myriad of problems. Once we start having predefined absolutes of what certain behaviors, facial expressions, or actions mean, we will no longer operate in healthy communication. Instead of communicating and discerning what we are experiencing, we will react out of our predetermined set of beliefs and move into some sort of self-protection. This can shut down intimacy, empathy, compassion, grace, discernment, and understanding. This may also cause people to accuse others of certain thoughts and motives inappropriately. They may then use those accusations as justification for setting an arbitrary boundary or consequence. If you have engaged in these behaviors, it is OK. You don't have to do it anymore. You have the ability to be present, communicate, ask questions, and discern.

A large part of maturity is taking personal responsibility for our own thoughts and emotions. This responsibility includes allowing others to have their own thoughts and emotions as well. There is such a freedom and peace that comes from no longer thinking other people's thoughts for them. I still remember the difference I experienced after receiving healing in this area. Just imagine for a moment what your life could be like if you could just be present in a situation, experience the peace and quiet of not hearing other people's thoughts, and enjoy the moment. This is actually possible. When we no longer waste our time being distracted and discouraged by thoughts and opinions we are projecting on others, it will increase our creativity, productivity, reasoning skills, and relational ability.

> Maturing into yourself means that you can now allow yourself to be present, experience life, and communicate in a healthy way.

If you have been thinking other people's thoughts, or others have been responding to you based upon their own perceptions of what you are thinking or feeling, know that freedom is available. It is healthy to take an honest look at any intellectual boundary violations in your life. Maturing into yourself means that you can now allow yourself to be present, experience life, and communicate in a healthy way. Remember, our team is available if you need help with this. You can do this!

CHAPTER TEN

Emotional Boundaries

Even the most stoic person experiences an internal emotional life. In the same way each one of us has our own thoughts, we also have our own feelings.

Even though our thoughts and emotions are two separate things, we need to understand that they are still directly connected to each other. Our feelings are an extension of our thoughts and beliefs. This may be why they get so confused and intertwined. Having emotional boundaries means that we each have our own joy, shame, fear, peace, guilt, and feelings of freedom. Even though we express our emotions in many ways, they only exist in *our* internal world. It can become problematic when different internal worlds collide and boundaries are violated.

Before we look at the different ways these boundaries can be infringed upon, let me affirm you—you have the right to feel however you want to feel. Your feelings are not wrong, and you are not wrong for feeling them.

As I was expressing that, I realize this is one of the ways our boundaries are violated. One of the ways our emotional boundaries are crossed is when we tell ourselves, or others, what we should or should not be feeling. There is not a predefined, correct set of emotions for each circumstance. Every person is processing trauma, loss, and circumstances their own way, through their own beliefs and experiences. None of us is going to be exactly the same.

We all have emotions and we will experience them no matter what we do.

I still remember the first time someone told me I was not wrong for feeling the way I felt. I think I was about 19 years old. That moment in time is stamped into my memory because it was such a huge revelation for me. I had grown up in a home where there was no room for my emotions, and if I expressed any of them, they were used against me. I can remember constantly being told how I should or should not feel, as well as being told that I was wrong for feeling certain ways. It was a very destructive environment of mental and emotional abuse. Being told that my feelings were not wrong, and that I was not wrong for feeling a certain way, shifted something in me. Although I did not pursue emotional health for many years, I am still grateful for that small gesture of grace.

This leads me into the next area of emotional boundary issues I want to talk about. Since I really wasn't allowed to have emotions growing up, I did everything I could to deny and numb them. The interesting thing about denying our emotions is that it never works! We all have emotions and we will experience them no matter what we do. Denying our own emotions, or anyone else's emotions, is a deeply destructive practice. It will lead to relational disconnection and pain. Denying our emotions keeps us from ever being able to confront them, process them, and get healing. I have found anger to be the most common mask for denying other emotions, but it leads to all sorts of unhealthy ways of trying to numb emotions instead of resolving them. In almost every situation where someone is attempting to deny their emotions, they end up being controlled by them instead. Denying our emotions is not beneficial. It will never help us resolve what we are emotional about. If this is something you have been doing, you now have the opportunity to feel your emotions and process what is actually happening. Being present in your emotions will allow you to learn self-control and be able to steward your emotional health.

One of the other ways we break emotional boundaries is by blaming others for our feelings. You will hear this in statements like, "You made me feel ..." The problem is that this is not really possible. Our emotions are always an extension of our own thoughts and beliefs. Maybe someone did something that inspired us to believe or think a certain way, and that caused us to feel a certain way, but only we have control over our emotions. The only way that someone else has control over our emotions is if we internally set the parameters for their words and behaviors to influence our thoughts and feelings. That would be an unhealthy intellectual and emotional system that we personally design. This is also how we end up letting external circumstances or situations have control over our emotions. This often leads us to blame and accuse other people or circumstances for the way we feel. This lack of personal responsibility can lead to destructive patterns in our lives. As we already know, blame comes from lies we believe about our own righteousness. If you have received healing in these areas, you are now empowered to take responsibility for your own emotions and discern why you are feeling them. This process will get easier as you practice.

Another way I commonly see emotional boundaries being broken is when people react out of what they think other people are feeling. It is so easy to assign certain behaviors or expressions as representing specific emotions. The problem is that this is not always true. People will express and share their emotions in many different ways. This type of misunderstanding can cause us to take responsibility for other people's emotions, become codependent, and begin to try to manage their feelings with our behavior. This type of manipulation will potentially cause problems in our relationships and will begin to allow our perception of other people's emotions to control our lives. If you have been engaging in this type of behavior and received healing in this area of your life, you will be able to establish healthier boundaries and allow other people to have their own emotional process. This may feel weird at first, and at times seem uncaring. Please understand this is the loving thing to do.

You are not responsible for anyone else's emotions, and no one else is responsible for yours.

One of the more destructive ways I see this type of emotional comingling destroy people's lives is when they believe they are discerning other people's feelings and trauma, but they are actually just experiencing their own feelings based off of their imagination of what they think about someone else's trauma. Sadly, this can put someone in a loop of spiritual battle that isn't theirs and that may not even really exist. This is one of the reasons it is so important to know our own identity and understand the difference between thoughts and emotions. It is extremely helpful to be present and capture our thoughts before they capture us and take us on an unpleasant emotional ride. It is good to remember that our emotions are telling us what *we* are feeling, not necessarily what other people are feeling.

In all of these scenarios, what can eventually happen is that we allow our emotions to define reality instead of being able to be present and discern what is happening. Many let their emotions confirm their thoughts about something, and then allow those thoughts and feelings to be their experiential reality instead of truly living their lives.

The beautiful thing is now that you have experienced healing, know yourself better, and can believe who you are, you can begin to establish healthy intellectual and emotional boundaries. You get to have your own thoughts and feelings, and everyone else gets to have theirs. You are not responsible for anyone else's emotions, and no one else is responsible for yours.

Anywhere you were intertwined with other people's feelings, you can now be free. Take the time to celebrate and allow yourself to mature in your newfound freedom. You have what it takes!

CHAPTER ELEVEN

Spiritual Boundaries

The things of the spirit are sometimes very abstract for our understanding which means spiritual boundaries can be even more unclear than emotional or intellectual boundaries.

As we are recovering from previous trauma and are maturing into our true selves, it is important to understand and implement spiritual boundaries. At some level, everything is connected to the spiritual realm. In reality, we cannot get away from that. In this chapter we are going to explore some aspects of boundaries in the spiritual realm.

The Scripture that came to mind when I was thinking about spiritual boundaries is in James:

> Let no one say when he is tempted, "I am being tempted by God," for God cannot be tempted with evil, and He Himself tempts no

one. But each person is tempted when he is lured and enticed by his own desire. Then desire when it has conceived gives birth to sin, and sin when it is fully grown brings forth death.
– James 1:13-15

One of the earliest revelations God gave me (in regard to the Identity Restoration concept) was this verse in James. He connected it to the enemy lying to Adam and Eve in the third chapter of Genesis. This is also why we have already looked at boundaries in our thoughts and emotions. Understanding and stewarding our thoughts and emotions is directly connected to our spiritual boundaries. Let's look at Genesis 3 in relation to the James verse.

But the serpent said to the woman, "You will not surely die (the father of lies introducing a lie). For God knows that when you eat of it your eyes will be opened, and you will be like God, knowing good and evil." So when the woman saw that the tree was good for food, and that it was a delight to the eyes, and that the tree was to be desired to make one wise (desire), she took of its fruit (conception) and ate (sin is birthed), and she also gave some to her husband who was with her, and he ate (fully grown). Then the eyes of both were opened, and they knew that they were naked (death).
– Genesis 3:4-7

As a new creation, we are kingdom-seekers by nature; it is who we are.

This is the basic tactic the enemy uses to entice us into sin and destruction. As a new creation, we are kingdom-seekers by nature; it is who we are. The enemy knows this, and he is constantly trying to entice us with things that seem like the kingdom of God. He offers them to us as quicker, easier, better, and more fulfilling. This tactic of enticing us to desire the things of the world through lies is how he tries to steal our identity, kill our authority, and destroy our community. Through these lies, the enemy lures us into a relationship with him where we conceive and birth sin that grows into death and the destruction of our lives.

There are two different kingdoms—the kingdom of God and the kingdom of the world. Having healthy boundaries in this area of our lives is essential to healthy growth. There are many ways these boundaries get confused. Here are a few of them.

One of the most common areas of spiritual confusion I experience with my clients is them not understanding the difference between their self-protections and demons. Now don't get me wrong, demons are real and they are a real problem. They are just usually not the problem we are dealing with. So often we have been trained through unhealthy religious teaching to assume what is happening is demonic. This is why mature discernment is so important. We will look at the importance of discernment in chapter twenty-six. So often, our own patterns, habits, behaviors, and old tapes that are running in our head get labeled as demonic attack. This will unfortunately cause us to battle with ourselves and cause even more trauma as we try to cast out a wounded area of our heart. A better approach as we are maturing into ourselves is to not assume anything and instead allow God to help us discern what is happening. Now that you have experienced healing, you will be able to discern more easily.

Speaking of demonic battle, this is another area where some of my clients have trouble. Getting information about something does not necessarily mean we are called to take it on as an assignment. This is one of the problems prophetic seers may experience. Just in case you are not familiar with this term, a "prophetic seer" is gifted with a greater ability than normal to see into the spirit realm. Often when

I work with seers, they are stuck in demonic battle that is causing relational, mental, and emotional issues for them. As in the natural world, just because you see something does not mean you need to act on it. Asking God what to do with the information is a healthier approach. I have helped many people who were stuck in the "second heaven" fighting demonic battles be able to transition into being present and living their life.

Prophetic feelers have their own challenges. Like seers, a "prophetic feeler" is gifted with a greater ability than normal to feel the things of the spirit. Many of the feelers I have worked with take what they are feeling and automatically make it a spiritual issue. This bypasses discernment altogether and does not allow for someone to know whether they are dealing with their own lies and wounds or a spiritual atmosphere. This again can put us in a position of battling ourselves and causing more personal and relational harm in the situation. The more we get to know ourselves and allow our hearts to have choices, the less this will happen. If you have experienced this type of emotional demonic battle, you can be free and learn how to steward your emotions.

Spiritual codependence is another area where we will violate boundaries. None of us can save anyone. Just like healing, salvation is a revelation of truth through spiritual discernment. Whether we are trying to make something happen for someone, control the environment around them, perform for them, or worry about their faith, we are not helping. Instead, this invites the enemy into the process and causes problems for us and them. This can cause all types of emotional, mental, and relational issues. Trusting God is a healthier approach. Choosing faith and believing God for other people's salvation and their faith walk will make everyone's lives better. Again, it is usually the lies we believe about our own authority that will cause us to be afraid for someone else's faith walk. If you have received healing in this area, you will begin to have trust, faith, and peace instead of fear.

Knowing the Word of God, the character and nature of Jesus, Holy Spirit, and Father God, along with our own identity in Christ, will give us clarity with spiritual boundaries. Taking the time to investigate and discern mentally, emotionally, and spiritually will help us mature and live a life filled with more freedom, peace, and joy.

Take your time; there is no hurry. You do not have to figure it all out right away. As you grow in maturity, this will allow you to know the good, perfect, and acceptable will of God. It will help you accept the things of the Spirit of God, find what is good, right, true, and pleasing to the Lord, abound in knowledge, and distinguish good from evil. This will empower you to be able to establish healthy boundaries between the kingdom of God and the kingdom of the world.

CHAPTER TWELVE

Physical Boundaries

Physical boundaries are probably the simplest to understand. It is much easier for us to comprehend how we cannot be in the same exact location and take up the same space as someone or something else. The issues with physical boundaries are a little different from the comingling that can happen in the other areas of emotional, mental, and spiritual boundaries.

There are some basic needs we have for our physical bodies that can be affected by unhealthy boundaries. Establishing healthy physical boundaries starts with having healthy mental, emotional, and spiritual boundaries. Resolving any codependent patterns we have in those areas will help us respect ourselves and others, as well as empower us to have healthy physical boundaries.

I have found that our acceptance and perceptions of the other non-physical boundaries are what inevitably establish the guidelines for our physical ones. That is why it is so important to be aware of and develop healthy practices in those areas.

As we have already looked at in the Awareness chapter, now that you have experienced some type of healing, you will be more aware of what is happening in and around you. Some of this awareness will include a new perspective on your boundaries. You may become uncomfortably aware of the dysfunctional emotional, mental, spiritual, and physical boundary violations in your relationships. This will create new challenges and opportunities for you.

Unresolved trauma and emotional, mental, or spiritual codependency causes some level of unhealthy physical boundaries. In this new space of awareness, you now have choices you didn't really have before. Now that you can be present, think your thoughts and feel your feelings, you can choose the physical boundaries that you believe are best for you. This could be a change in direct physical contact or proximity to others.

Unfortunately, our self-protections help us stay in unhealthy circumstances or relationships because we've learned to cope with abuse. These coping mechanisms sometimes keep us from being aware of the dysfunctional mental, emotional, spiritual, or physical abuse. Becoming aware of, and addressing, any direct abuse can be extremely difficult and, in some cases, dangerous. Hopefully, you are not in a dangerous situation. For those who are not in dangerous situations, changes can be made without serious issues. If you are in a physically dangerous situation, I recommend that you get whatever professional help you need to be safe. You do not deserve to be treated that way!

Even if we have trouble establishing and maintaining them, our physical boundaries, regarding direct contact to our body, are fairly simple to understand. We get to decide who or how people have access to us physically. Where it may begin to become more abstract is when we start looking at physical boundaries regarding location, time, and action.

Navigating your boundaries is based on your capacity, not other people's needs.

You not only have the right to decide how people have access to your physical presence, but you also get to decide where you go, what you do, and for how long you are available. This is where physical boundaries can begin to get a little muddled. Again I will remind you, if you have not worked out the other non-physical boundaries you will have difficulty managing these. Navigating your boundaries is based on your capacity, not other people's needs. There is a never-ending need in this world. If you want to be effective and helpful, taking care of your needs first is the most important part.

Now that you have experienced healing and know yourself a little better, you will understand your personal needs better as well. Your physical boundaries start with your needs and your capacity. Part of healthy physical self-care includes having boundaries that do not cause undue harm to ourselves.

Now that you are more aware of yourself and your needs, it may be beneficial for you to review your boundaries regarding location, time and action. A good way to do this may be to ask yourself some questions.

Let's start with location. What I mean by location is that you have permission to decide where you physically arc, where you go, and why. Some questions you could ask yourself are:

Why am I here?

Does God want me to be here?

Do I want to be here?

Do I need to be here?

Is it safe for me to be here?

Do I have the capacity to be here?

Is it beneficial for me to be here?

Why would I go there?

Does God want me to go there?

Do I want to go there?

Do I need to go there?

Is it safe for me to go there?

Do I have the capacity to go there?

Is it beneficial for me to be there?

Now let's look at time. What I mean by time is that you have permission to decide how much time you are available for someone or something. Some questions to ask yourself about time could be:

Does this still give me time for myself?

Does this still leave time for my needs?

Do I want to commit to this amount of time?

Do I have the capacity for this?

Do I have time for this in my schedule?

The last aspect of physical boundaries I want to review is action. What I mean by action is you have permission to decide what you physically do, or how you help or serve others. Some questions you could ask yourself are:

Why am I doing this?

Does God want me to do this?

Do I want to do this?

Do I need to do this?

Is it safe for me to do this?

Do I have the capacity to do this?

Is it beneficial for me to do this?

These are very simple questions. You could ask yourself these questions, or any others you come up with, to see whether or not you have healthy answers.

If you find you have healthy answers you are happy with, celebrate that and continue living in freedom, peace, and joy. If you find you have some unhealthy or codependent answers, I recommend you discuss them with God and pursue freedom in those areas of your life. There are plenty of boundary resources available to help you. If you cannot easily resolve these boundary issues, I recommend processing with a counselor or an Identity Coach.

You matter, your physical health matters, and you have permission to be free and enjoy your peace according to your needs, capacity, and boundaries.

CHAPTER THIRTEEN

Taking New Territory

I believe that in order to have healthy relationships and healthy relational boundaries, we have to start with developing a pattern of good intellectual and emotional boundaries. If you have had trouble with these in the past, you should find it a little easier now that you have experienced your healing encounter. It is good to remember though, we are all on a journey. As we begin to establish new healthy boundaries, we may become aware of more areas where we need healing. That is OK. Let yourself experience the freedom you have, and do not focus on the areas where you may need more healing. You can address that area once you take ownership of the healing you have experienced.

It reminds me of when God shared the process of entering the promised land in Exodus 23. He shared that not all the land would be cleared out right away. Little by little in a way they could steward, the Lord would give them new territory. As they took the new land, they were to drive out the inhabitants and make no covenant with them or their false gods. This is the same thing we need to do with everyone who has been inhabiting our thoughts and feelings.

> I will not drive them out from before you in one year, lest the land become desolate and the wild beasts multiply against you. Little by little I will drive them out from before you, until you have increased and possess the land. And I will set your border from the Red Sea to the Sea of the Philistines, and from the wilderness to the Euphrates, for I will give the inhabitants of the land into your hand, and you shall drive them out before you. You shall make no covenant with them and their gods. They shall not dwell in your land, lest they make you sin against me; for if you serve their gods, it will surely be a snare to you."
> – Exodus 23:29-33

Just as the Israelites needed to increase and possess the land, we need to grow into the fullness of ourselves and own our healing. The beasts of fear, the false gods of shame, and the inhabitants of guilt all need to be driven out. The patterns, habits, traditions, and routines of our old unhealthy relationships and behaviors all need to be conquered and removed from our lives.

If it is not freedom, peace, and joy—it is not normal.

We have all had teachings, trainings, and mindsets drilled into our head since we were young. Not all of these are healthy or helpful. Some of these have become so familiar that we don't even realize they are an outside influence. We have accepted them as normal. If it is not freedom, peace, and joy—it is not normal. If these false-normals are not driven out, they will multiply against us, ensnare us, and cause us to sin against God. We now can erase those old tapes and drive out the wild beasts of fear, shame, or guilt that have multiplied against us.

Conceptually that sounds great, but you may be asking, "How do we practically do this?" That is a good question! To be honest, it is something I am still working through. I have spent years driving out the old, unwanted inhabitants of my thoughts and feelings that were established through cultural influences, generational false beliefs, and traumatic experiences. I will share with you what I have learned through working with my clients over the years, as well as partnering with Jesus in my own journey.

One of the key tools I have developed over the years to help my clients walk out their freedom is the Three Steps to Life. This tool is designed to help you be present, choose reality, and experience God. The simplicity of this concept has helped some of my most wounded clients begin to experience freedom, peace, and joy in their lives. If you want more information about this life-changing tool, I break these steps out in detail in chapter five of my book *Identity Restoration*, and in week four of the online course. Let's review them here.

Step One - Intentionally Stay Present

What I mean by this is to stay connected and present with yourself and your situation. This is a less common practice than you may think. So often, instead of living in the present moment, we will not only just live in the past or the future, but we will also choose to trigger off into some sort of self-protection in the way of fear, shame, or guilt. This can cause us to not truly be present, and instead of being able to engage in the moment and respond, it is more like we are just observing and reacting.

Staying present mentally and emotionally will help you to have the capacity to remove yourself from a situation if needed. It will also allow you to establish boundaries and healthy communication where needed instead of perpetuating a dysfunctional pattern. There has to be intentionality to this because of the many self-protections we have established that are distracting us from being present.

> Staying present mentally and emotionally will help you to have the capacity to remove yourself from a situation if needed.

Step Two – Choose Reality

What I mean by choosing reality is to let yourself think your thoughts and feel your feelings—to actually acknowledge what it is you are thinking and feeling. So much of what is going on internally is ignored. We tend to automatically just accept whatever is going on in our thoughts and feelings as reality, without even stopping to check what they are. We can trust our feelings to tell us what we are feeling, but we cannot trust our feelings to tell us what other people are doing, thinking, or feeling. We need to capture our thoughts and pay attention to how our thoughts are affecting our feelings in a situation.

We cannot just accept how we feel as an accurate read of what is happening; although we can trust those feelings to help us find out what we believe is happening. Other than loss, if we are personally feeling an emotion that doesn't fall in the categories of righteousness, peace, and joy, we are most likely believing a lie. A lie about God, ourselves, others, or the circumstance. The process of letting ourselves be present in the situation and aware of our own thoughts and feelings is critical to establishing healthy intellectual and emotional boundaries. When we can begin to realize that we have our own thoughts and feelings that may or may not represent the situation, we can begin to understand how other people have their own thoughts and feelings. This will allow us to start driving out other people's thoughts and feelings from our own.

Step Three - Connecting with God

What I mean by connecting with God is to align yourself with the reality that God is already with you. This third step is the process of allowing yourself to acknowledge the presence of God however He is revealing Himself to you in that moment. Let yourself be in the presence of God. This will allow you to engage with the Lord and bring Him into your thoughts and feelings right in the situation or circumstance that you are actually experiencing.

These three steps are the foundational process of establishing new, healthy boundaries. As you begin to understand the boundaries and the differences between your own thoughts and emotions, you will be able to establish new communication habits and relational boundaries. The new healthy habits, patterns, traditions, and routines you establish will help you increase and possess this new territory.

CHAPTER FOURTEEN

I Think – I Feel

We have looked at intellectual boundaries and emotional boundaries with others, now we are going to look at the boundaries between our own thoughts and emotions. This is probably one of the most confusing areas of boundaries that my clients are working through.

Everyone has thoughts and feelings. They are a normal part of life. The problem is, sometimes they are so familiar to us, we tend to not be conscious of them. Often, my clients are unaware of the thoughts they are thinking, the emotions they are feeling, or even the difference between the two. The internal processes that are happening have become so ingrained in them; it is almost like they are now just background noise in a foundational reality they are not even aware of. This can cause continual loops of unhealthy occurrences they do not necessarily want to experience. Becoming aware of our thought processes and emotions is a huge step in the development of change and freedom because with it comes the power to choose.

The first step in healthy communication and healthy relationships is learning the differences between our thoughts and emotions. One of the reasons that emotions can get the best of us sometimes is because we do not understand or even know what we are actually feeling. When we can know and understand clear boundaries in our own thoughts and emotional life, we will begin to be able to establish healthy boundaries with other people's thoughts and emotions. This will allow us to establish healthy relational boundaries with them as well.

We can't capture a thought we believe is a feeling.

The strongholds, arguments, imaginations, lofty opinions, and elevated false identities we have established in our thoughts have caused us to experience fear, guilt, and shame.

> For though we walk in the flesh, we are not waging war according to the flesh. For the weapons of our warfare are not of the flesh but have divine power to destroy strongholds. We destroy arguments and every lofty opinion raised against the knowledge of God, and take every thought captive to obey Christ.
> – 2 Corinthians 10:3-5

These strongholds, arguments, and lofty opinions are not an attack from the enemy that we need to spiritually defeat. They are our own personal thoughts we need to capture. Understanding this will help us tear them down. If we don't know the difference between our thoughts and emotions, we will have trouble capturing our thoughts. We can't capture a thought we believe is a feeling. We have divine power to be able to reconsider our thoughts, change our thinking, repent, and believe the good news of freedom, peace, and joy.

To help understand this better, let's look at the meaning of some of these words.

Strongholds:

The Greek word used for stronghold in 2 Corinthians 10:4 is Strong's G3794, ochyrōma. It means: A castle, stronghold, fortress, fastness, the idea of holding safely, anything on which one relies, reasonings used to defend your position.

The strongholds are the things we are personally holding on to for safety, and the positions we are defending. The reasonings we have used to create and defend our positions, strongholds, and fortresses keep us hiding in fear. There are demonic agreements and influences with these strongholds, but they are not demonic strongholds. They are strongholds of our own unhealthy thoughts and beliefs.

Arguments:

The Greek word used for arguments in 2 Corinthians 10:5 is Strong's G3053, logismos. It means: Computations, reasoning, imagination, judgements, and decisions.

The arguments are the imaginations, reasonings, and judgments we use to prove our positions and decisions right. These are more of an offensive, rather than defensive, tactic we use to defend our positions and blame in fear.

Lofty opinions:

The Greek word used for lofty opinions in 2 Corinthians 10:5 is

Strong's G5313, hypsōma. It means: An elevated place or thing, a barrier, a high thing.

The lofty opinions are the barriers, the false idols, and the false identities we elevate above the knowledge of ourselves and God. These are the things we look to for identity and hope that are not God, not true, and cause us to cover ourselves in shame. These strongholds, arguments, and lofty opinions are what we have the divine power to tear down.

The problem comes in when we misunderstand these and begin to label them as feelings. When we do this, we are unable to connect with what we are actually feeling, and we will react out of an imagined lofty stronghold instead of reality. When we can properly define thoughts, we can get in touch with the real emotion and find out what the belief system is that is creating the feeling.

The example I use in chapter five, Three Steps to Life, in my book *Identity Restoration* is a situation where it seems like you may be experiencing manipulation. I used manipulation because it is such a common unhealthy communication tool. A lot of my clients have expressed similar situations and they described that they felt manipulated. The issue is that manipulation is not an emotion. It is a thought. What can happen is that a familiar feeling can get associated with a particular type of situation where you think you may have experienced manipulation. This thought of being manipulated can then get labeled as an emotion you are feeling. Then when you experience a certain situation, you will "feel" manipulated. This is a real problem because it may be happening or may just be a perception. Either way it can cause you to react out of an unresolved trauma from the past, instead of being able to be present and respond out of who you are. This will keep you from being able to find out the real feeling and resolve the trauma.

When we can steward our thought life, we can then steward our emotions.

Emotions are almost always an expression of our thoughts. When we can know the difference between thoughts and feelings, it can help us to capture our thoughts and make them obedient to the truth. When we can steward our thought life, we can then steward our emotions. The problem is not that our emotions are out of control, it is that our thoughts are out of control. It is ineffective to attempt to manage our emotions without managing our thoughts. Usually, even though there are some exceptions (such as loss), when we are emotionally overwhelmed, it is our thoughts running rampant and creating strongholds of fear, arguments of guilt, and opinions of shame.

When you experience healing, you will become more aware of the difference between your thoughts and emotions. If you are having trouble defining the difference between them, help is available. An Identity Coaching session will help you take inventory of your heart, discover your thought processes, help you understand your structures of defense, experience your emotions, and find out what truth is available for you. You can get to know yourself and give your heart a choice.

Freedom is available.

Peace is possible.

Joy is real.

CHAPTER FIFTEEN

Getting To Know Yourself

Getting to know our personal boundaries, needs, likes, and desires is such an important aspect of our maturing process. Unfortunately, many of my coaching clients have had trouble making decisions because they do not really know themselves and express to me that they are unaware of what they even like or really want.

It is exceedingly difficult to establish emotional, intellectual, or relational boundaries when you do not know yourself. As we looked at in the Establishing Boundaries chapter, if you do not know yourself, you cannot really know your needs. In this chapter we are going to explore the discovery process of getting to know ourselves.

Now that we are more aware of the differences between our thoughts and emotions, as well as other people's thoughts and emotions, it will be much easier to get to know ourselves better. When we have the freedom to explore, test, and experience life without managing other people's thoughts and feelings, we can become aware of what we really think and feel.

Personal responsibility can be very scary, or very exhilarating, as we begin living our life based on our own choices, needs, desires, and boundaries. Sometimes this can be a new experience for you. If you've had a pattern of analyzing how other people think and feel about what you are doing or saying, there will now be a newfound freedom. In this freedom is where you get to explore, try new things, make mistakes, and learn what you like and do not like.

Mistakes are not sins.

Just think for a moment what it would be like if you were able to make choices without any thought of relational retaliation, emotional punishment, or accusations. What if you could actually believe that your heart is good, you make good choices, you are trustworthy, and you have God's and others' interests in mind? What if you aren't selfish just because you also have needs? What if you could live a life and have boundaries based upon your needs and your capacity? Wow, what could that look like?

You have permission to make mistakes. This is a good thing too, because if you live your life, you will make mistakes. As you try new things, you will find that they are not all things you like or want. That is OK; that is how we learn. You may also find that things you have been doing because you "should" be doing them, aren't things you like or want to do anymore. That is OK also.

I have been around the religious community enough to know that some of you may be triggering from what I am sharing. The idea of trusting yourself and following your heart can be challenging for some. Let me be clear—I am not saying to go live a lifestyle of sin and reject all your responsibilities in life. Mistakes are not sins. Let your childlike wonder be restored and allow yourself to follow the desires of your heart—your newly redeemed, alive, righteous, fruitful, pure, and accepted heart. If you have trouble with this concept, my *Who Do You Think You Are?* Bible study may help you. You can also schedule an Identity Coaching session if you need help getting to know your heart and your true identity in Christ.

> Finally, brothers, whatever is true, whatever is honorable, whatever is just, whatever is pure, whatever is lovely, whatever is commendable, if there is any excellence, if there is anything worthy of praise, think about these things. What you have learned and received and heard and seen in me—practice these things, and the God of peace will be with you.
> – Philippians 4:8-9

As a new creation, the natural desires of your heart will be true, honorable, just, pure, lovely, commendable, excellent, and worthy of praise. If you are having desires that are not honorable, just, and pure, that is not your heart; that is a lie and a wound. Your new heart in Christ is trustworthy.

> Delight yourself in the LORD, and He will give you the desires of your heart.
> – Psalms 37:4

The Greek word used for delight in Psalms 37:4 is ānag (Strong's H6026). It means: To be soft, pliable, luxurious, delicate, to delight.

Now that we have experienced healing in our hearts, we can softly, luxuriously, and delicately be pliable and able to delight in the Lord.

As we can be vulnerable with God and trust Him and the truth of who He created us to be, He will give us the desires of our hearts. This area of trust, softness, and delight is where we will get to know ourselves. We will discover what we truly like, what we enjoy doing, and what we were gifted and called to do. We will begin to experience the natural expression of who we are.

As we get to know ourselves better, we will begin to adjust our boundaries. These new boundaries will be based on our needs and capacity, not another person. This is not selfish; this is permission to exist, live, and thrive. Having healthy boundaries is better for everyone we are in relationship with. If we don't have healthy boundaries, we will end up interacting with others through a self-protection of fear, shame, or guilt instead of being present. This will keep us from knowing ourselves or the others we are engaging with.

As your heart softens for the Lord and you begin to delight in Him, allow yourself the permission to be pliable and adjust your boundaries. It is OK that you won't get it all right all the time—it will be a learning process. You will get better at this and you will mature into yourself. You can do this. Let yourself try, make mistakes, learn, try again, and grow.

I have a few questions to help you see how well you know yourself, and to help you get to know yourself better. Please take a few minutes with each one of these questions to think about them and let yourself dream.

What are the things that bring me peace?

What are the things that bring me joy?

What are the things that bring me freedom?

What do I enjoy doing the most?

What is my favorite form of creative expression?

Now, let's ask God a couple questions. Let yourself ask the Lord these questions and give yourself room to receive.

How can I make more room for these in my life?

What boundaries need to be modified in my life to help me?

CHAPTER SIXTEEN

Self-Nurture

As followers of Jesus, self-nurture is a potential conundrum. After all, aren't we supposed to deny ourselves and carry our cross? This is something I see many followers of Jesus struggle with. How do we deny ourselves and nurture ourselves at the same time?

> Then Jesus told His disciples, "If anyone would come after Me, let him deny himself and take up his cross and follow Me."
> – Matthew 16:24

> And He said to all, "If anyone would come after Me, let him deny himself and take up his cross daily and follow Me."
> – Luke 9:23

Obviously, the Lord wants to express something here in His Word. In two of the gospels, the Scripture is telling us to deny ourselves. How do we nurture ourselves in a way that denies ourselves?

> ## Self-nurture is the process of caring for, encouraging, and stewarding your own growth and development in the Lord.

Unfortunately, there has been a lot of confusion around this topic. This causes people to have an unhealthy perspective about denying their own needs and only focusing on others. This perspective contributes to many relational and emotional issues in our lives.

Self-nurture is the process of caring for, encouraging, and stewarding your own growth and development in the Lord. This is a key factor in the process of maturing into yourself. I do not think we can fully mature without caring for our own needs. So it makes sense that we need to find an understanding of who or what it is we are being told to deny. This reminds me of an encounter I had one time when I was hearing a lot of teaching around the idea of denying ourselves daily and carrying our cross.

I was listening to Scripture and praying about this whole discipleship concept of "denying myself and carrying my cross" when the Lord drew me into a vision with Him. If you are not familiar with what I mean by "vision," it is what Peter experienced in Acts 10:9-16. It is a spiritual, emotional, intellectual, and visual encounter that happens in your mind's eye that experientially seems just like real life. My encounter started with Father God entering the room with me and asking me a question. He asked, "How many times was Jesus crucified on the cross?" This alone was an overwhelming experience for me. I could have stopped there and just have been filled with the revelation of Jesus and the completeness of His sacrifice for me, but God had more. Right after the Father asked me this, Jesus entered the room and said, "Everyone follows Me into death, not everyone follows Me into life ... Discipleship is following Me into life." I was undone! This was such an impactful moment for me, I get emotional almost every time I recall it.

In that moment things became more clear to me. The "self" we are to deny is our old, dead self that was hostile to God and is no longer who we are. Carrying our cross daily is the continual reminder that the old self died on the cross with Jesus. It is not an attempt to crucify the new self. If we are to follow Jesus, we need to deny our old "dead self," remind ourselves that this is no longer who we are, and follow Him into His abundant life as a new creation. This is discipleship. Our new self, with our new heart and new spirit, is redeemed, alive, righteous, fruitful, pure, and accepted. We can allow ourselves to be loved, known, trusted, pleasing, powerful, and to have a purpose. We need to nurture our new self and allow ourselves to live, grow, and mature into the stature of the fullness of Christ.

So how do we care for and encourage ourselves? To start with, I would recommend that we follow David's example in 1 Samuel 30:6 and "encourage and strengthen ourselves in the Lord." Right in the middle of a horrific trauma, before doing anything else, he encouraged himself in the Lord.

> And David was greatly distressed, for the people spoke of stoning him, because all the people were bitter in soul, each for his sons and daughters. But David strengthened himself in the LORD his God.
> – 1 Samuel 30:6

The Greek word used for strengthened in 1 Samuel 30:6 is ḥāzaq (Strong's H2388) Some of its meanings are: To fasten upon, encourage, be established, fortify, help, mend, repair, strengthen, be sure, take hold.

If we cannot love ourselves and allow ourselves to be loved, we can neither love God nor others.

David strengthening himself in the Lord is a commonly referenced Scripture in describing how to handle distress. As we look at some of the fuller meaning of the word used in the passage, we can see that David encouraged, established, fortified, helped, mended, repaired, and strengthened himself in the Lord. David needed to nurture himself in the Lord so that he was able to inquire from the Lord and help others.

The Great Commandment tells us to love God and love others as we love ourselves. Commonly, this gets whittled down to just love God and love others. So often, the concept of loving ourselves is missed, or even directly rejected. The problem with this is, we must let ourselves be loved in order to love God. We love because He first loved us. If we cannot love ourselves and allow ourselves to be loved, we can neither love God nor others. Often, what I see happen with people who do not love themselves is that they will use others, or allow themselves to be used, in an attempt to feel loved. This is another way that we destroy our relationships.

Commonly, the idea of self-nurture and taking care of your needs is looked upon as selfishness. This is not selfishness; this is healthy discipleship. If we don't take care of ourselves, like David did, we won't be able to take care of others. Not loving ourselves or not letting ourselves be loved, is the selfishness. The problem with this is that selfishness keeps us from getting our real needs met. If we love, care for, and encourage ourselves in the Lord, we will be able to have our real needs met and will naturally help others with their needs.

Refusing the lie that we are still that old, dead self is one of the ways we can love ourselves. Choosing to believe we are a new creation in Christ is one of the ways we can love God and ourselves. We are not trying to nurture the old, dead self. We are accepting our true identity in Christ and allowing ourselves to be loved and nurtured. When we can love God and love ourselves, we can delight in Him and He will fulfill the desires of our hearts.

There are multiple aspects of self-nurture. We are going to explore some of our physical, mental, emotional, and spiritual needs in the next few chapters. We will look at how you can nurture yourself in these areas so you can love God and love others. Accepting that you have permission to nurture, encourage, strengthen, heal, repair, and fortify yourself in the Lord is the beginning of this process. God cares for you, and He wants you to abide and be nurtured in His love. You are worth it, and you can do this.

CHAPTER SEVENTEEN

Self-Care - Physical

Physical needs may not be the first thing that comes to mind when we think about mental and emotional healing. It is something that really needs to be considered in our maturing process. We are holistic beings, and our physical, mental, emotional, and spiritual health are all connected. As we continue to look at self-nurture, we must explore the need to care for ourselves physically.

Over the years, I have noticed how the emotional and mental pain and trauma of my clients was affecting their health. I have also noticed how they would sometimes experience physical healing along with their mental or emotional breakthrough. This, along with my own research and healing, has changed the way I do Identity Coaching. I now see how the physical is so intimately connected to our mental and emotional health. This has led me to incorporate the awareness breathing techniques into my coaching sessions that I have learned in my own therapy sessions and personal research. This allows my clients to engage and connect with their parasympathetic nervous system to process and release any trauma stored in their body. This allows for a physical, mental, emotional, and spiritual alignment with truth. If you have experienced an Identity Coaching session, you are familiar with this.

I have seen so many physical healings happen through prayer and coaching sessions. Some have been creative miracles, and some have been healings related to the processing of unresolved trauma. Personally, I do not care how God does it, I just love watching the healing happen! I have seen Crohn's disease reversed, broken bones reset, migraines disappear, back pain resolved, brain fog cleared, eating disorders broken, irritable bowel syndrome vanish, food and seasonal allergies gone, and even cancer disappear. It never stops being amazing.

You may or may not have experienced a tangible physical healing when you had your healing encounter. Whether you are aware of it or not, I believe there is some level of physical healing along with the emotional or mental breakthrough. Now that you are more free, the attention to your physical health will benefit your maturity, as well as your ability to steward your thoughts and emotions.

It is not faith to ignore or deny an issue.

Let me be clear—I am not an expert on physical health, and this is not intended to give you medical advice. As part of your holistic maturity, I do recommend you get the medical advice you may need. It is not faith to ignore or deny an issue. If you are aware of some physical abnormality in your body, find out what it may be from a qualified person. Part of the ability to physically nurture yourself is to know what your physical condition is and what your body needs. Getting advice from someone more qualified on the subject is a really good idea.

If you experienced physical healing during your encounter, there will be a process of maturity in your body as well. Regardless of what the issue was, you do not have the experience of operating in proper physical health in that area of your body. You may need a type of physical therapy to learn how to live your life with your new healed reality. You will need patience and practice to do this. Thankfully, you have the fruit of the Spirit in you.

Caring about the physical health of our bodies is a healthy and mature mindset. This type of mindset is not something I have always had. As a kid I was so wounded and confused that I could not even comprehend the idea of caring about my body. I was just surviving and trying to numb the emotional pain I was living in. I still remember a time in my early teens when I was talking with a neighborhood friend about drugs. She told me that she would not do drugs because she cared about her body too much. I still clearly remember this conversation because it was such a weird concept. I could not even connect with the idea of caring about my body or myself in a nurturing way. I had no respect or understanding of how my actions and lifestyle were affecting my body or even that it mattered in any way. It was years later before I had any sense of stewarding and caring for my physical health. Our physical health matters, and you have permission to live healthier.

There are many ways that we can nurture ourselves physically as we continue to mature. Unfortunately, any one of these could have been distorted by our unresolved traumas and could have been twisted into a self-protection that was adversely affecting our bodies. For example, our need to eat and fuel our bodies could have become an infatuation or a self-comfort that caused damage to our bodies. For me, food has always been a self-comfort. I still must pay attention to this. I am now aware that the enemy used food against me, and I would unsuccessfully try to use it to manage my emotions. Others may have experienced a different type of disordered eating. If you experienced healing with any food related issues, you now need to develop a healthier relationship with food and nurture yourself with it instead of using it as a self-protection or self-comfort. This could similarly apply to physical exercise, medications, sleeping, rest, or other physical areas of your life. Wisdom, moderation, understanding, and grace are needed in all these areas.

Ignoring our physical needs is not maturity.

Ignoring our physical needs is not maturity. Part of the process of maturing into ourselves is taking personal responsibility for our physical health. The inability to care for and nurture ourselves physically is the evidence of immaturity and the need for mental and emotional healing.

I recommend you do some research in the area of need you have and make a plan to bless and nurture yourself physically. Let yourself get the rest you need. Find a way to move your body that fits your personality and lifestyle. Learn the foods and nutrients that are right for your health. Get a massage or go to the spa and treat yourself. Go see a physical therapist or chiropractor if it is appropriate for you. Schedule that doctor's appointment you have been putting off. Just give yourself permission to manage the care of your body. If you don't know how to do it, let others help you. Get the specialized help you need. It is OK to need help.

CHAPTER EIGHTEEN

Self-Care – Mental

Mental self-care is a vital part of our maturity. What I mean by mental self-care is to intentionally nurture and develop your intellect and your thought life in a way that brings you peace, joy, and freedom. It is personally investing in yourself and pursuing the healthy desires of your mind—learning, growing, and maturing. This will look a little different for each one of us.

As we looked at in the Intellectual Boundaries chapter, one of the most important aspects of mental self-care is to have healthy boundaries with our thoughts. In that chapter, we explored the concept of personal responsibility in thinking your own thoughts and allowing other people to think theirs. I believe this is one of the most important things you can do for your mental health.

My academic background is limited. I could barely read growing up and was dyslexic until I came to faith at the age of thirty. I was never officially diagnosed and did not recognize the severity of the problem until it was healed. That healing opened me to a whole new world of reading that had been difficult for me before. When I was younger, I was totally uninterested in school, saw no real benefit in education, and cheated in most of my classes to make up for my reading issues. Math was the only subject that was easy for me.

I share this with you to show that mental self-care can have its challenges. We may have limitations or disabilities that make things more difficult. You have your own challenges and limitations that are different than mine. For me, even getting healed from the symptoms of dyslexia did not fix all my issues with reading. I was healed, but God did not backfill the experience. I am still a slow reader, and I do not have a love for it like some of my friends and family. I read for specific, informational purposes. It is not a comforting or relaxing time for me. I prefer to listen to books rather than read them. Even when it comes to time in the Word, most of the time I am listening to the Scriptures, not reading. Thankfully, there are usually ways around our limitations.

Finding ways to stimulate your intellect is important to your cognitive health.

The point is, now that you have experienced a healing encounter, there are areas of your mind that are immature and ready for growth. Finding ways to stimulate your intellect is important to your cognitive health. Since I am not an expert on this, I recommend researching beneficial ways that work for you, your lifestyle, and your desires.

There could be old desires and interests that were shut down because of your unresolved trauma that you now have renewed interest in. Maybe there are things you have been wanting to learn, but your previous fear, shame, or guilt kept you from pursuing them. Maybe there is a language you have thought about learning, a musical instrument you have been wanting to play, or a class you have been wanting to take. There may be some games you have been wanting to learn to play but have not let yourself. Games are a great way to intellectually stimulate our minds. There could be a project in your home that will challenge your current knowledge or skill level. Learning and developing new skills is a great way to grow and mature. Now may be the time to do it.

Opening our minds up to new or different ideas outside of our understanding is vital for our maturity. Discussing ideas with someone who sees differently, and letting ourselves relate to how other people think, is so good for our development. I still remember early on in my faith as I was reading the Scriptures and getting revelation about what is now the foundation of my ministry. My friends were at various places on the spectrum of faith. I would talk and discuss these ideas with them and allow myself to understand their point of view. This helped me to refine and develop what I do now. It helped solidify what I do believe and gain understanding of the things I don't. If I had only let myself hear, study, and talk to people who agree with what I already thought and knew, it would have been a dangerous limitation that could have stunted my growth.

A common attack from the enemy that I have seen in my client's lives is an attack on their intellect. Accusations of stupidity are something many need to process through and be healed from. Sometimes these attacks were orchestrated by people who were close to them. I know this one personally. From patterns of abuse and accusations in my childhood, I believed I was stupid. I still remember when I first began to question that. In high school, while I was struggling to read, not applying myself, not studying, partying, and barely ever doing my homework, I was still doing better on tests and with my overall class grade than some of my friends who were trying to do well. This confused me! I remember thinking, "How can I be stupid if I am doing better than they are?" This was not resolved until much later in my life. I still had many old tapes of accusation and discouragement playing in my head. I did begin to question the accusations of my past and the ones I had in my own thoughts. After years of pursuing healing, and allowing myself to grow intellectually, I can now accept and admit that I am intelligent. Even though I still don't really know how to spell, and I am learning grammar as I write and edit my books.

You are free to learn without condemnation.

You now have freedom in your intellectual abilities that you may not have had before your healing encounter. You are free to learn without condemnation. Free to make mistakes and not be punished for them. Free to try new things and grow in understanding. In my opinion, one of the best tools for learning is trying something, failing, and making mistakes. Talk about experiential revelation! You have permission to try. You have permission to make mistakes, learn, try again, and get better at whatever it is you are learning.

If you find yourself in a continual loop of making the same mistakes, it is most likely another area of unresolved trauma that needs healing, not an intellectual issue. With many of my clients, and in my own life, I have seen these loops become ammunition for accusations against our intelligence. The enemy will commonly use this tactic to lie to you and attack your mental health in an attempt to keep you from healing. If you find yourself in these types of loops, I recommend pursuing additional healing.

Learning is just one of the aspects of mental self-care. Training yourself to think in a healthier way is also a large part of it. As you are growing in your intellectual health and your thought life, one of the aspects of your maturity is your intellectual focus. From the very beginning of your life, the enemy has been trying to get you to believe lies and think in unhealthy ways. Now that you are free from some of the denial and unhealthy thought patterns, you can begin to focus on and steward your thought life. The psychological world calls this meta-awareness, or metacognition. This is an awareness of our thought processes and an understanding of the patterns behind them, as well as deliberate attention toward the contents of conscious and subconscious thought.

One of the ways I see this is like a carnival of thoughts. There are many different loops of thought rides we can take at any time. As we are walking through the carnival of our mind, we can be aware of the different rides, without having to get on them. Even if we catch ourselves on one of those rides, we can get off that ride any time we want. We do not have to take that loop to its destructive end. We can capture that thought and bring it into the light. Becoming aware of our thought patterns and taking responsibility for them is a significant benefit in the maturity process.

You have permission and divine power to decommission those unhealthy thought rides and tear down those strongholds. As you discontinue those old structures, you can rebuild new, healthy thought patterns.

> Finally, brothers, whatever is true, whatever is honorable, whatever is just, whatever is pure, whatever is lovely, whatever is commendable, if there is any excellence, if there is anything worthy of praise, think about these things. What you have learned and received and heard and seen in me—practice these things, and the God of peace will be with you.
> – Philippians 4:8-9

You can do this. You can think differently. Thinking on what is pure, lovely, commendable, excellent, and worthy of praise is an aspect of your new identity in Christ. You were created to be able to learn. You have everything you need to grow and mature.

CHAPTER NINETEEN

Self-Care – Emotional

If you aren't focusing on your emotional self-care, you're missing out. Believe me, you want to get really good at this! It is an important part of maturity and healthy relationships.

What I mean by emotional self-care is to intentionally nurture and develop your emotional health in a way that brings you peace, joy, and freedom—to allow yourself to acknowledge, accept, make space for, and express your emotions in a healthy way. This will be an ongoing learning experience that looks a little different for each one of us.

As with intellectual boundaries, one of the most important aspects of emotional self-care is to have healthy boundaries. Emotional boundaries will help you take responsibility for your own emotions and allow other people to be responsible for theirs.

Learning emotional health has been a long and ongoing process for me. Growing up in a home where there was no room for my emotions made it difficult to mature in them. The lack of training created a void where I did the best I could by developing a variety of unhealthy patterns of denial, numbing, and deflection. The most common pattern was masking almost all the painful emotions I was experiencing with anger. I was not aware this was a self-protection system I had created; it just seemed like normal life for me. My inability to make room for the painful emotions helped me to accept the unhealthy lifestyle of anger. I am still working on deconstructing some of the old unhealthy structures I built. Hopefully, what I have learned along the way will be helpful for you.

One of the challenges I have personally had in my emotional maturity is that I have bipolar 2 disorder. Unfortunately, I went most of my life with this being undiagnosed. I always thought I was in the bipolar camp, but I didn't think I was diagnosable because I was only aware of bipolar type 1, and that didn't fit my symptoms.

After the traumatic loss of our home from a fire in July 2018, my mood swings got worse. I was no longer able to manage my moods by simply stewarding my thoughts. Pursuing healing for my attention and emotional issues led to my diagnosis in March of 2021. I share this to let you know that we all have our own challenges we need to conquer in our emotional health journey.

Emotions are not a result of the fall.

One of the best places to start with our emotional self-care is to accept that we are emotional beings, and we will have feelings. I have worked with so many people who express that they are not emotional people.

I have found this to be untrue for everyone who claimed it. Except for very rare and specific mental and personality disorders, we all experience emotions. You have emotions and feelings. If you need to, take a moment to let that sink in. Our job is to learn how to accept and steward them if we want to experience healthy lives and relationships.

Emotions are not a result of the fall. They are a God-given resource for us to be aware of our relational, mental, and spiritual health. They are like instruments on the dashboard of a car. They give us a reading of how things are going under our hood. That is why it is so important to start with emotional boundaries—acknowledging our feelings, and accepting they are ours. This will allow us to address whatever issues are being reported to us. Our feelings are a great guide to let us know what we are perceiving, thinking, and experiencing. If we are unable to honestly acknowledge our emotions, we will tend to blame other people and circumstances for them. Making room for our emotions will help us find out what we are thinking that is creating the emotion. Painful emotions come from either lies or loss. If we refuse to accept the emotion and confront it, we will never be able to find out if it is a loss we need to grieve or a lie we need to repent from.

As we allow ourselves permission to have emotions, and be aware of them, we will begin to have the ability to steward them in a healthy way. I have found for myself, and with many of my clients, it seems easier to have empathy and compassion for others than it is to have them for ourselves. A good tool to see where we personally need empathy, compassion, and healing is to take notice of the areas we usually find ourselves connecting with other people's trauma and emotions. If we are not aware of our own emotions in these situations, we tend to be codependently connected to other people's feelings instead. As we become present in our emotions, we can then have empathy and compassion for ourselves. Just like the Word mentions in Matthew 7 and Luke 6, we need to address the emotional log in our own eyes before trying to help someone else with the emotional speck in theirs.

There is an additional dynamic to the need for emotional empathy and compassion for ourselves. I have found it extremely helpful to not only have a sense of empathy for our younger selves who experienced the emotional trauma, but to also have it for our present self in the moment. Having an understanding that we were a young child at some point and experienced trauma is somewhat easy to have empathy for. But it doesn't seem to be as easy to have empathy for ourselves in the present moment as an adult who is still experiencing the emotional trauma. It is essential to acknowledge both. If we can validate our emotions and have empathy for both our younger self and for our present self, we can then process the issue and find healing. Doing just one or the other can be incomplete and keep us in a place where we still act out of the unresolved trauma.

There are many ways we can help ourselves experience and mature in our emotions. One of the tools for being present and stewarding our emotions is an exercise I learned in therapy called diaphragmatic breathing. This tool has many more benefits than just for stress and anxiety. This full lung breathing exercise will help engage your parasympathetic nervous system and allow your body to slow down, rest, and connect with your thoughts and feelings. Using this breathing technique, along with the Three Steps to Life in chapter five of my book *Identity Restoration* will help you immensely in your journey of maturity. As we become aware of our emotions, we will become more aware of our thoughts. If you remember, our emotions are an expression of our thoughts. We will then be empowered with the opportunity to repent and believe the good news. Along with awareness, we also need to give ourselves permission to express our emotions. As we are working out our emotions, having a safe outlet to express them is invaluable.

Some additional practices that are beneficial to our emotional health are physical exercise, forgiveness, healthy eating habits, managing our self-talk, cultivating hobbies, experiences, and relationships we enjoy, focusing on intentional gratitude, and giving ourselves permission to make mistakes. This will greatly impact our ability to steward our emotions. If we can look at our emotional health in combination with our physical, mental, and spiritual health, we will be much more balanced in our lives. There are multiple resources online to help you learn and grow in your emotional health. A simple way to start could just be searching "emotional self-care" online.

You have permission to feel, and you have permission to pursue a healthy lifestyle of freedom, peace, and joy.

CHAPTER TWENTY

Self-Care - Spiritual

Spiritual self-care, also known as spiritual disciplines, is such a necessary aspect of our maturity. Without it, do not expect to mature into your true self emotionally, mentally, or spiritually.

What I mean by spiritual self-care is to intentionally nurture and develop your spiritual health in a way that develops your relationship with the Lord and brings you peace, joy, and freedom. As holistic beings, our spiritual, emotional, mental, and physical health are all tied together. If we want to fully mature into our true selves, we need to address all aspects of our being.

As I worked on this chapter, it became abundantly clear to me that this is an area of my life that needs some maturity. I have been working on my emotional, mental, and physical health to catch up with my spiritual health, and I ended up dropping some of the spiritual disciplines in the process. To be honest, I have been evaluating the health of some of the religious practices in my life for a few years now. The trauma of the fire and the stirring of my mood disorder helped to make my spiritual walk a little messy.

Spiritual disciplines can sound rather daunting, but in reality, they are just expressions of our faith and life with the Lord. That is why I like to think about it as spiritual self-care. As we care for ourselves spiritually, we are expressing the different nuances of our relationship with God and our identity in Christ. In the same way we need to approach our maturity in a holistic way, I believe we need to nurture our spiritual relationship holistically with Jesus, Holy Spirit, and Father God. I have found if we have an unbalanced approach, we will have an unbalanced spiritual life. In this chapter we are going to explore the different ways we can nurture and develop our spiritual health and relationship with the Lord.

The purpose of focusing on our spiritual self-care is not to get better at each of the disciplines but rather to grow and mature in our relationship with God.

I want to share with you some of the different aspects of what I have found helpful in having a balanced approach to growing our relationship. Your process may look different, and that is OK. Each one of us needs to walk out our faith in the relationship we have with the Lord. In no particular order, the aspects we are going to explore are community, communion, worship, meditation, Word, prayer, giving, serving, fasting, gratitude, forgiveness, and repentance. Let's look at each of these individually.

Community:

> For as in one body we have many members, and the members
> do not all have the same function, so we, though many, are one

body in Christ, and individually members one of another.
– Romans 12:4-5

Relationship and community are key components of our spiritual care. One of the ways we experience love is by having our needs met. We build each other up and encourage each other in community. Some of, but not all, the spiritual disciplines require some level of community to be able to express them. We are all part of the body of Christ, and we each serve our different purposes together as one body. We love and are loved by each one of us expressing our faith, serving one another, and taking care of each other's needs. There are many ways we can connect and do life together. There is no specific way we need to do this. To be a body though, there is a necessity to be connected in some way. As we grow in maturity, we will naturally desire connection and relationship with others. I highly recommend pursuing a faith-centered, nurturing community.

Communion:

The cup of blessing that we bless, is it not a participation in the blood of Christ? The bread that we break, is it not a participation in the body of Christ?
– 1 Corinthians 10:16

I see communion more as an expression of the recognition, acceptance, and celebration of the Lord's provision any time I am engaging in eating or drinking, rather than a tradition we must do as part of a liturgy. It is such a humbling and grounding experience to intentionally take the time with Jesus and others to join in the remembrance of His sacrifice, death, resurrection, and future return. It is an incredible practice to remember Him. At whatever level of tradition or liturgy you prefer, communion will inspire spiritual growth.

Worship:

> I appeal to you therefore, brothers, by the mercies of God, to present your bodies as a living sacrifice, holy and acceptable to God, which is your spiritual worship.
> – Romans 12:1

Years ago, I was reading this Scripture, and I felt the Lord revealed to me that the foundational aspect of worship is agreement. The demonstration of worship is the expression of that agreement. This comes in so many more forms than just music and singing. There is something special about corporate "worship." Whenever I have long spans of time without Sunday morning church gatherings, corporate worship is the thing I miss most. I really recommend finding ways to express your agreement with the Lord and experience His presence.

Meditation:

> Let the words of my mouth and the meditation of my heart be acceptable in your sight, O LORD, my rock and my redeemer.
> – Psalms 19:14

Meditation is simply a time of resting in the Lord and intentionally focusing on His presence. This allows us to take our experience with Him beyond an intellectual thought of Scripture and into an experiential revelation of His truth. Letting ourselves engage our senses physically, emotionally, mentally, and spiritually in our relationship with God will help us to mature into the fullness of who we are in Christ. This can be as simple as practicing the presence of God in our day to day lives or spending time in prayer. If you need help with this, the Three Steps to Life, along with the breathing techniques, will help you tremendously in this process.

Word:

So faith comes from hearing, and hearing through the Word of Christ.

– Romans 10:17

Almost all my encounters and visions with God were inspired from a time of study in His Word. The Word of God is so important in the development of our relationship with Him. As I mentioned, most of my engagement with the Word of God is through audio. I have an audio Bible on my phone and computer, a Logos Bible study program, and the blueletterbible.org that I commonly use for time in the Word. Almost all the Scripture I use and quote is ESV. I use NKJ and ESV for study. The audio versions I use are NIV, NLT, and ESV. I recommend finding a way to spend time in God's Word in whatever way works with you, your needs, your challenges, and your personality.

Prayer:

For I know that through your prayers and the help of the Spirit of Jesus Christ this will turn out for my deliverance.

– Philippians 1:19

I have found that it is hard to have a relationship with someone you do not communicate with. Prayer is a relational conversation with the Lord. As we converse with Him, I recommend that we speak and listen. So often the listening piece is missing in the relationship. Hopefully, now that you have experienced some healing, you are able to listen more and trust that God is engaging with you. Unfortunately, so many of my clients have been religiously trained to discount, deny, or rationalize away God's part of the prayer conversation. I recommend establishing an ongoing prayer life where you communicate with the Lord and make space for Him to communicate with you.

Giving:

> You will be enriched in every way to be generous in every way,
> which through us will produce thanksgiving to God.
> – 2 Corinthians 9:11

Finding a way to express your agreement with God and invest into the kingdom through giving is such a glorious growing opportunity. Each one of us has been created to pursue and fulfill the desires of our hearts. Letting ourselves be part of different expressions of kingdom development through giving helps us experience that fulfillment. Whatever your compassion and your calling lead you to, I recommend finding ways to invest into others who have needs that you care about.

Serving:

> As each has received a gift, use it to serve one another, as good
> stewards of God's varied grace.
> – 1 Peter 4:10

Allowing ourselves the opportunity to express our God-given gifts and talents to serve others is good stewardship. It allows us to get to know ourselves better and mature in our gifting. As we examined, one of the ways we love each other is by taking care of one another's needs. Using our gifts to serve will help us to experience and understand love, as well as prepare us to receive love. I recommend finding ways to express your compassion and love through your spiritual gifts.

Fasting:

> And they said to Him, "The disciples of John fast often and offer
> prayers, and so do the disciples of the Pharisees, but yours eat
> and drink."
> – Luke 5:33

I have found fasting to be one of the best reset buttons in my life. It affects my physical, mental, emotional, and spiritual health. I highly recommend implementing fasting into your lifestyle in a way that is healthy for you and your needs. The benefits can be immeasurable. It is always wise to discuss this with your doctor before you begin.

Gratitude:

> Give thanks in all circumstances; for this is the will of God in Christ Jesus for you.
> – 1 Thessalonians 5:18

As we heal from our previous trauma, an intentional attitude of gratefulness will help train our thinking to focus on the good things we have. This is not about denial; it is about focus. We still need to be honest with ourselves and with God about what we are thinking and feeling as we also practice focusing on the things we are grateful for. We can retrain our brain in a way that will bring us freedom, peace, and joy. Whenever I apply this, it is helpful to my attitude and emotional health.

Forgiveness:

> Be kind to one another, tenderhearted, forgiving one another, as God in Christ forgave you.
> – Ephesians 4:32

Forgiveness is a key component to a lifestyle of freedom. Letting go of offenses and debts we think people owe us is essential to maturity. Unforgiveness is a toxic problem that will develop a mindset of bitterness and keep us from experiencing freedom. I highly recommend reviewing chapter seven of my book *Identity Restoration* if you have any questions or issues with forgiveness.

Repentance:

> The time is fulfilled, and the kingdom of God is at hand; repent
> and believe in the gospel.
> – Mark 1:15

Now that you have experienced healing and freedom in your life,
you will have the ability to choose. You can reconsider what you are
thinking and have the freedom to believe the truth. This is what it
means to repent. In my opinion, this is one of the most powerful
practical actions you can do to impact your life and your maturity. If
you can change your thinking, you can change your life.

I hope this is helpful for you. As with any religious practice, these
can all be taken out of context and become a meaningless ritual or
legalistic ammunition. It is very important to remember that these
are all intended to help nurture your relationship with God and allow
you to live in freedom, peace, and joy. For freedom Christ has set you
free. Stand firm in your freedom and don't submit to another type of
slavery.

CHAPTER TWENTY-ONE

Building Faith

Almost every client I work with talks to me about their desire to develop their faith in the Lord and their trust in Him. It seems this a struggle for many. Personally, I know this is one of my greatest struggles. Often, after watching God continually meet people in the depths of their lifelong pain and hurt, and miraculously comfort them, heal them, love them, and restore them to the truth of who they are in Him, I am dumbfounded with the level of unbelief I still have. It amazes me that I can live such a supernatural life and still not fully trust God. My ability to compartmentalize my relationship with God is unsettling to me. It is a constant journey of growth. Sometimes I feel victorious in this journey, and sometimes I feel defeated—but I press on and do not quit.

Let's start out with a simple definition of faith from Scripture. If we are going to build something, it seems appropriate to know what it is we are working on. In Hebrews, God's Word tells us that faith is being sure of what we hope for and certain of what we do not see. Being sure and certain of our hope—Christ in us, the hope of glory. What a hope! Think about that for a minute. Are you sure and certain of the glory of Christ in you? That truth alone can build your faith. If you are able, let yourself meditate on Hebrews 11:1 and Colossians 1:27, and let your heart and mind ponder the idea of the hope and glory of Christ in you.

While on this journey, there are a few things I have learned that have helped me grow in my faith. Hopefully they will help you. As we continue in our maturity process, faith will be a key factor in our growth.

> So faith comes from hearing, and hearing through the word of Christ.
> – Romans 10:17

If faith comes from hearing and hearing the Word of Christ, His Word needs to be a significant part of our faith development. As I have shared previously, almost every significant encounter I have had with the Lord started with studying His Word. The Bible is such a beautiful gift to us. As we looked at in the spiritual-care chapter, time with God in His Word is essential in our growth. We have access to God's Word through reading the Bible and through direct revelation from Holy Spirit. Now that you have experienced some level of healing, hopefully you are in an even better position to receive truth from Holy Spirit. There are two Scriptures that I thought of that help us understand Holy Spirit's role in hearing the Word.

> These things I have spoken to you while I am still with you. But the Helper, the Holy Spirit, whom the Father will send in My name, He will teach you all things and bring to your remembrance all that I have said to you.
> – John 14:25-26

When the Spirit of truth comes, He will guide you into all the truth, for He will not speak on His own authority, but whatever He hears He will speak, and He will declare to you the things that are to come. He will glorify Me, for He will take what is Mine and declare it to you. All that the Father has is Mine; therefore I said that He will take what is Mine and declare it to you.
– John 16:13-15

As we look at these Scriptures, we can see that the Holy Spirit is our helper and teacher. He is reminding us of everything Jesus said, guiding us into all the truth, and glorifying Jesus by declaring to us the things of God. In 1 Corinthians, His Word tells us that our understanding of the things of God come through spiritual discernment. So Holy Spirit is teaching us the things of God and helping us understand them through spiritual discernment.

If we want to build our faith, we need to listen to Holy Spirit every way He is speaking to us.

Even when we are reading the Bible, the understanding only comes through spiritual discernment. It is always Holy Spirit teaching us. We are not figuring it out on our own. This process of spiritual discernment can happen in many ways. We can receive truth from the Bible, in prayer, hearing a sermon, talking with a friend, in a dream, encountering God in a vision, or intentionally allowing ourselves to be aware of His presence. Regardless of the experience, listening to Holy Spirit so we can hear the truth is needed. He can talk to us through thoughts, impressions, visions, feelings, memories, sensations, circumstances, an audible voice, and even our imagination. He can meet us anywhere we are and reveal truth in whatever way we need. Now that you have experienced healing, you may find you are more receptive to these different ways God is communicating to you. Take the time to explore these, discern His truth, and grow in faith.

If we want to build our faith, we need to listen to Holy Spirit every way He is speaking to us. It never stops amazing me how God meets people in the specific way they can understand. Unfortunately, the world, the culture, false religion, and our traumatic experiences have trained us to discount or not even be able to receive God's Word from Holy Spirit. Most of the time we do not even have the faith to listen so we can grow in faith. It has taken me a long time to trust the voice of God in my life.

In the beginning of my journey of faith, I met Jesus and started following Him in a visual encounter. I have experienced revelation visually in my mind's eye, intellectually through prayer, emotionally through confession, and even audibly through hearing God a few times. He has fully engaged my intellect, my emotions, my senses, and my imagination in multiple ways. He is not limited. If you are having trouble relating to the different ways of spiritual discernment, I recommend an Identity Coaching session to be able to encounter God, get to know your true identity, and give your heart choices.

Now that we can listen to Holy Spirit in every situation, let's look at some of the practical ways we can build our faith. One of the kingdom principles I see throughout God's Word is the concept of remembrance. Even the John 14:26 verse we looked at talks about Holy Spirit bringing all things Jesus said to our remembrance. From early in the Bible, God instructed His followers to establish memorials of remembrance, celebrations, feasts, and traditions—all to remember. Remembering the truth and the work of the Lord will help stir up faith.

I recommend finding ways to create memorial stones of your faith journey and your healing journey to celebrate the work of God and your growth. Be creative and let yourself have some tangible memorials that will remind you of what God has done in your life. This could be anything, even an actual stone. Let them be an expression of your faith. I also recommend finding ways to celebrate. Just like the feasts and the holidays, let yourself celebrate the good things God has done in your life. Build new traditions of celebration in your life to remind you of the truth you are grounded in and the healing you have experienced.

A lot of the principles we looked at in the emotional, intellectual, and spiritual self-care chapters will help you as well. Capturing every thought, bringing them into the light, repenting, believing the truth, speaking that truth over yourself, and encouraging yourself in the Lord will all help. Celebrate the truth and declare it in faith! As you build your faith, you will recognize the fruit of the Spirit and the gifts of the Spirit manifesting in your life. This as well will build your faith. As the Lord works in you to will and to work according to His good pleasure, it will continue to build your faith.

> Does He who supplies the Spirit to you and works miracles among you do so by works of the law, or by hearing with faith?
> – Galatians 3:5

Galatians 3:5 tells us that the Lord supplies the Spirit to us and works miracles among us by hearing and faith. Celebrating those miracles and remembering them will continue to build your faith.

Trusting the Lord releases supernatural power into our lives and circumstances that was always available but not always active. Trusting God is what completes the circuit and allows that supernatural power to flow. Allow yourself the space and the time to remember and celebrate the memorial stones of your journey.

In the next three chapters, you will be hearing from a few of our coaches. Each will share insight from their area of experience in hopes of providing other perspectives on maturing into yourself. First will be our Identity Coach, Heather Wright, sharing her insights on believing in yourself. The next will be with our Dreams Coach, Colleen De Silva, sharing her insights on allowing yourself to dream again. Then, our final guest chapter will be from our Recovery Coach, Laura Burwick, sharing practical steps to live in wholeness.

CHAPTER TWENTY-TWO

Believing In Yourself

by Heather Wright

One of the most powerful keys to experiencing the transformational grace of the Holy Spirit, once you've received the truth of your identity from Jesus, is to choose to believe it. Now that you've come through the other side of your healing encounter and the part of your identity that had been opposed by the adversary has been restored to you, own it! As you engage in the process of seeing yourself the way you really are, you will grow into it.

This may sound simple, but as you've been learning in your journey through this book, it isn't easy. Believing in yourself as revealed to you by Jesus won't automatically be familiar. It can even seem daunting. But the good news is many have gone this way of maturing before you and can point the way for you to follow. Paul found the need to give these helpful tips to the believers in Ephesus who must have also been trying to grasp how to live their lives from their true identities.

...when you heard about Christ and were taught in Him in accordance with the truth that is in Jesus. You were taught, with regard to your former way of life, to put off your old self, which is being corrupted by its deceitful desires; to be made new in the attitude of your minds; and to put on the new self, created to be like God in true righteousness and holiness.
– Ephesians 4:21-24 NIV

As we consider putting off the old and putting on the new, our tendency can often be to focus on the actions that might be required, i.e. habits we need to replace, new skills we need to learn, etc. While these are helpful and necessary for the full expression of our true self, solid, lasting belief in ourself is an inside job. If the sole focus is changing our outer expression without a change of inner perception, we tend to find ourselves performing and pretending (faking it 'til making it) and that incongruence yields frustration and self-doubt. If this happens, don't fret—it's normal. And it's merely a signal to you that the potential is there and you are ready to bloom in this area of your life. All you need is practice to expand your mind.

Paul provided this recipe for change in the middle of this sandwich in Ephesians 4:23—the secret sauce is **"to be made new in the attitude of your minds"** and again in Romans 12:2 (both NIV), **"Do not conform to the pattern of this world, but be transformed by the renewing of your mind. Then you will be able to test and approve what God's will is—His good, pleasing and perfect will."**

Jesus made sure to emphasize that it all boils down to what is happening in our minds when He taught about how to transform the current manifestation of things in Mark 9:23 (NKJV): that **"All things are possible to him who believes."** By flipping our focus from changing what we're doing to what we're believing, we'll find all the necessary ingredients fall in place to yield the lifestyle of our true selves.

What you believe will determine the thoughts you are thinking.

The Recipe for Transformed Living

Beliefs – Thoughts – Feelings – Choices –
Actions/Words – Habits/Patterns

What you believe will determine the thoughts you are thinking. What you think about determines how you feel. The emotions you feel release chemicals that will bring positive or negative effects in your brain and body that will lead you to make choices and to take action accordingly. Over time this recipe becomes a neural pathway in your brain, propagating the programming of your nervous system, and is reflected in the patterns you're living in. For the purpose of creating the way of life of the true you, this recipe looks something like this:

When you believe in yourself as you truly are, your thoughts will tend to be empowering, which will give you feelings that are freeing, peaceful, and joyful, leading you to choose words and actions that support the true you.

"Out of the abundance of the heart the mouth speaks."
– Matthew 12:34 ESV

With practice, this will become your new pattern, or habit of living. That's the kind of confidence that will remain strong and stable no matter how anyone else responds. That's the kind of confidence Jesus walked in regardless of any circumstance, always believing in Himself, and it's available for you too!

The Practice of Believing in Yourself

One of the most effective ways to practice believing in yourself is by starting with a clean slate when you first wake up in the morning. Most of the time we have a moment before we remember the "stuff" from the day before— the time when we first breach consciousness, before we pick up our phones or put our feet on the floor. Neurologically, it's at this place that the neurocircuits of your brain are in their most pliable state to be transformed, so grab this moment to allow yourself to engage with Holy Spirit in renewing your mind. You may likely find that thoughts about your day will begin to flood in, and when this happens, just let them go on by like they are passing by on a train. Also let go of any prior perceptions of yourself that conflict with seeing yourself in your true identity. Now you are ready to imagine and create with Holy Spirit what it's like to be the true you. Let yourself be curious. Enjoy just hanging out with Father, Jesus, and Holy Spirit. Here are some questions you can ask God and yourself as you explore:

What do I value most as I look at life from this new facet of who I am?

How does this aspect of me reveal God to the world?

Knowing this is who I am, what am I drawn to doing?

Let yourself absorb it all. Then begin to bring it back to your present day by asking,

What will be my main focus today, given this is who I am?

What will I say yes to?

What will I say no to?

What will I wear?

What will my posture be?

How will my voice sound when I speak?

What will I choose to talk about?

How does that feel?

According to my favorite cognitive neuroscientist, Dr. Caroline Leaf, all you need is seven minutes a day of thinking thoughts that lead to pleasant emotions and within 21 to 66 days you will have created a new neural pathway in your brain. Once that occurs, being your true self will be familiar and normal. Be sure to give yourself grace in this process; transformation is never a straight line. If the old perceptions about yourself crop up, simply thank them for showing up to remind you that is not who you are! Celebrate the wonder of even the smallest ways you see that "belief in the true you" beginning to shine through. If it's for one minute, celebrate that minute. Don't worry about the other minutes. With continued practice believing in you, reminding yourself who you really are, the minutes you sustain the true you will expand.

When you sincerely believe in yourself from the heart, your life will be a catalyst for inspiration and change for the lives of others around you and God will be glorified! The unfolding process of "you" can be delightful, peaceful, and fun. It's happening perfectly. Enjoy it!

CHAPTER TWENTY-THREE

Dreaming Again

by Colleen De Silva

"I want you to tell the world that I AM fun." – Holy Spirit

Allowing ourselves to dream again after a healing encounter can feel brand new and even uncomfortable at first. Feeling uncomfortable doesn't mean it's wrong. It just means that we are stepping into new territories and unfamiliar lands with God. When we go to new places, we have to walk around and get familiar before we feel like it's home.

The concept of dreaming includes nighttime dreams, visions, and aspirational/life dreams. First, let's consider maturing into our aspirational/life dreams.

After a healing encounter, our hearts are more open to the impossible and we are willing to be honest in the present. So many times, we realize that what we thought we wanted and enjoyed isn't really what we want and enjoy anymore. We can also realize that what we want, but didn't think we could have, is actually what God wants for us too. In both situations, we end up having to reevaluate and *dream again*.

My story is that I had always secretly wanted to be a film actor. I could never justify this as a Christian but when I went to a ministry school, I had several healing encounters and decided to try this acting thing out. I was asked to act in a short film playing a villain. I still struggled with feeling ashamed, but I chose to take the role. I stepped into new territory.

On the day of filming, I finally invited Holy Spirit into this new world. I told Him I was feeling ashamed and afraid to fail. Then, I heard Him respond, "Sweetheart, you are going to do great." I continued, "I don't know how to be a villain. Will you please help me?" Then, to my surprise, He said, "Why don't you slowly drag a chair around the character. It will scratch the floor to intimidate and scare him." What?! I thought He'd say something like, "You're on your own kid," or "I don't want you to play a villain." No, He gave me advice. I experienced God's partnership in my acting dream.

What we carry and the dreams we desire are important.

Since then, Holy Spirit has given me more acting advice and amazing revelations. One in particular convicted me to never put God in a box when it comes to dreams. After the premier of a short film I acted in, I heard about an audience member having a breakthrough in the area of grief. While she watched the film, she felt at peace with her father's death and was able to let the trauma and pain go. After hearing this, Holy Spirit said, "Colleen, the breakthrough that you carry emanated through the screen and brought breakthrough to her." What she didn't know is that I too had lost my dad, and that I had experienced breakthrough and healing during filming.

What we carry and the dreams we desire *are* important. We may not understand how they all fit together but that's not our responsibility to know. Ours is to be like little children and walk with Jesus through the uncomfortable feelings of stepping into new territories. It's where we discover even more about God, who He created us to be, and what gifts we carry. Maturing into ourselves is an ongoing process and it takes childlikeness to grow. Maturing does not mean that we lose our childlikeness. In order to dream again, we have to become like children!

Jesus said to the disciples after they asked Him who is the greatest in the Kingdom of Heaven, **"Truly I tell you, unless you change and become like little children, you will never enter the Kingdom of Heaven."** (Matthew 18:1-3), Children are free from worry, they wait for their guardians to guide them ... to tell them it's dinner time, time to do homework, time to go to bed. They listen and obey. What do children do when they aren't sleeping, eating, and learning? They are PLAYING! This is so important because children really do know how to have fun, don't they?

As Christians we forget this part of childlikeness. We make excuses as to why we don't follow the dreams God has planted in our hearts, or if we pursue them, we are ashamed and feel the need to justify them. When we were children running around and playing, not once did we justify playtime, we begged for it! As children, we automatically felt permission to be joyful and free. Do you find yourself justifying your actions when you are doing something you love or enjoy? "I am going to have a spa day because I need it for this reason and that reason ... oh and ... God told me to do it. So, I'm good ... I think?"

You're not alone! The majority, if not ALL, of Christians have spoken something similar. It's as if we think that being a Christian is all sacrifice and no play. If this were true, then why did Jesus die for our sins and send the Holy Spirit? A beautiful Spirit who is love, *joy*, peace, patience, kindness, goodness, faithfulness, gentleness, and self-control. All of these are good things and **"against such things there is NO law"** [emphasis added] (Galatians 5:22-23). Jesus sent a fun Holy Spirit to guide our days and to hang out with us all the time! When I asked Holy Spirit what He'd like me to focus on for this chapter, I heard Him say, "I want you to tell the world that I am fun." He *is* fun and wants to have fun dreaming again with us!

Has anyone ever asked you to tell them what your perfect day would look like? A perfect day that has no constraints or impossibilities? This question allows you to dream without the fear of time or age, lack of money, family expectations, or anything else! I encourage you to ask yourself what your perfect day would look like. Invite Holy Spirit to sit with you as you write it down and ponder. Be very honest with yourself. Then, ask Holy Spirit and yourself what you believe that is preventing you from having this perfect day? This is a practical way to catapult you into dreaming again with Holy Spirit.

We *were* meant to LOVE our life, to enJOY what we do, to have PEACE in the process, to PATIENTLY wait for God's best, to be KIND to ourselves and others, to receive GOODNESS, to FAITHFULLY dream for the impossible, to receive gentleness and be GENTLE with ourselves and others, and last but not least, to use SELF-CONTROL because we are powerful human beings. Let's experience dreaming again by taking small steps, even in the uncomfortable, and watch God's miracles happen as we dream again.

Dreaming Again After a Healing from Fear

How many times have you heard others or yourself say, "Fear is not your friend"? I say this to myself at times when I fear the future, the moment, the lack, and more. I remind myself that my friend is not fear but Love, God's love, His hope for the future, and all that He encompasses.

Fear is a debilitating concept. I say concept because that is what it is. A lot of times we get healed from our fears after having the revelation that fear is merely a concept. We find that the fear does not actually produce what we expect, or if it does, it usually fixes itself and we are able to get right back up and move forward.

In the acting world, I've heard a lot of people say that if you don't have fear then you don't care (I actually dislike hearing this—yuck). Then you have the other side, where people say if you go in there fearless, you'll blow them away. Well, make up your mind! I see why people justify the fear, it is probably soothing, but what can happen is that people begin to partner with the fear. They "use it" and welcome it as a friend, when fear is the opposite of God's nature, which is love.

> So do not fear, for I am with you; do not be dismayed, for I am your God. I will strengthen you and help you; I will uphold you with My righteous right hand.
> – Isaiah 41:10

If God is commanding us to not fear, then we are not to fear regardless of what culture or others tell us. When fear is lifted off, there is a new world around us. There are new opportunities to dream again. This too may feel difficult at first because we are maturing into our new fearless selves.

One great tool that has activated me to dream bigger is to write down one hundred dreams. These dreams can be as simple as a new couch or as complex as a person's miracle healing. It is a list to make consisting of one hundred dreams/hopes/aspirations you desire. This tool is a great second step to the "perfect day" activation. The "perfect day" imagination brings your mind to the possibilities, then the "one hundred dreams" list causes you to dig deeper and find all the things you dream of, even if they are small, big, seemingly impossible, or simple.

The first time I ever wrote down my one hundred dreams, it was hard. I had thoughts that sound like, "I don't need this," or "I'd be fine if this didn't happen," or "I don't have one hundred." I did the activity anyway. The key idea of writing these dreams down is to invite God to fulfill them. We may strive towards dreams but there is a time and place where God wants to simply give those dreams to us. I find He likes to bless us and give us happy surprises.

God can and will do anything. He truly loves us and the more we open ourselves to asking Him, the more we can receive from Him. That is the goal of this "one hundred dreams" list. It activates us into a new level of dreaming again, and dreaming again is trusting Him with child-like hope and faith. It is not easy to hope and have faith, but it is valuable and very rewarding when we get to see the result of our faith instead of striving into dreaming again. Fear gets proven wrong, and we get to have fun with Holy Spirit.

Dreaming Again in the Night

I am a huge fan of nighttime dreams. I fully believe that God loves to talk to us in the night while our physical bodies are sleeping, and our spirits are awake. I also believe those dreams or nightmares can be either brushed away or used to reveal the plans of the enemy. God is purposeful; he uses the night for uplifting, informing, guiding, and bringing us to Him.

Maybe you are someone who has never had a dream or nightmare before, or you never remember your dreams. Maybe you are someone who dreams every night. Either way, if you ask for more dreams and steward those dreams, your nighttime dreaming will shift! You may have more detailed dreams or remember them more. Now, this all sounds fun when I talk about it, but sometimes it can be uncomfortable to suddenly have some weird dreams, and it can be easy to just push those dreams aside and say, "That was just a pizza dream." Even so-called "pizza dreams" can bring you closer to God.

You may also feel overwhelmed with all the new revelation you are receiving. I suggest you record your dreams even if they seem ridiculous and invite Holy Spirit to show you what they mean or if you are processing something. If you have a nightmare, ask God what He has to say about it and what He wants to do with the nightmare. Recording your dreams can look like writing down key moments that were highlighted to you or using your voice recorder on your phone to quickly say what you saw. You can have a folder online or in your computer to type up your dreams too. Most importantly, inviting the Holy Spirit as you process your dreams will open up even more healing, encouragement, closeness, and revelation than ever before.

I've actually developed a journal to record your dreams, *Your Dream Journal.* It includes common definitions, steps and tips to help get started, and an example of how one can record their dreams within the journal.

Nighttime dreaming is a great way to mature into ourselves, asking the Holy Spirit who we are, whose we are, what our giftings are, and what season we are in.

Ways That May Keep Us from Dreaming Again

One of the biggest lies and ways that can keep us from dreaming again is believing it is too late. There are many times I have to combat this myself and trust in God. There are also several of my clients who either say this or God brings it up in a session. The enemy likes to tell us we are too old, we missed our chance, or that time is running out. So, we get in a rush and feel overwhelmed, or we feel either unqualified or overqualified due to age or experience. This can hinder our dreams of being parents, married, artists, athletic, career driven, retired, and so much more!

The big question is how do we continue dreaming again without letting those lies and hopeless thoughts hinder our progress and peace? One way is to get with God and listen to His truth constantly. When we receive healing, we must steward what truths were given to us. This will keep us turned to Him and not those lies, whether they are old ones we threw away or brand new ones that get thrown at us.

God is supernatural and He holds time in His hands (Psalm 31:15). So we aren't too old and it isn't too late. We didn't miss our calling because certain opportunities didn't work out. He has not forgotten our dreams or forgotten us. He keeps all His promises. He sees you and me. The more we mature into ourselves each day, the more we will grow in knowing and trusting Him and His timing. Then our desire to pursue the dreams that once seemed impossible will burn even brighter. We will take bigger risks and not let anything hold us back from trusting ourselves and God with dreaming again. **"Trust in the Lord with all your heart and lean not on your own understanding"** (Proverbs 3:5 NIV).

Conclusion

My hope for you, the reader, is that you read this chapter and feel encouraged to dream again. To push yourself forward and not give up on dreams from the past or present. To know that God will never stop surprising you with His love and showing up for you. I hope you rediscover and explore dreams that you thought were too far gone or too impossible. My prayer is that you will see them come true!

Hope deferred makes the heart sick, but a desire fulfilled is a tree of life.
– Proverbs 13:12

I declare that this is a season for you to see those trees of life flourish and grow in your life. We are meant to always be maturing and dreaming, so keep discovering! Soon you will look behind you and realize how far you've come.

CHAPTER TWENTY-FOUR

Practical Steps To Wholeness

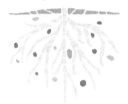

by Laura Burwick

I remember in the beginning of my healing journey as an adult, feeling that I would never be complete. I had given my life to Jesus as a teenager but had no idea what that meant, and no one taught me. I was brought up in a Lutheran church. My parents made sure we went to Sunday school and to church on Easter and Christmas. I don't think they understood that a personal relationship with Jesus was possible. They took me and my brothers because culturally it was expected and because that was their understanding of Jesus and church.

I remember the day I was confirmed and gave my life to Jesus. Something in my heart and spirit really understood the commitment. It felt really special to me. I asked the pastor if I could pick out two of the hymns for the service. He said I could, and I picked one for each of my parents based on their favorite hymns. It was a very important life event to them, and I wanted to honor them. I remember feeling that I was really coming alive inside and was filled with anticipation. After the day was over, the feeling faded and nothing really changed in my life.

My first kiss and the first time I experimented with cigarettes was at my church youth group. I remember feeling so disconnected and confused about what had happened and I felt ashamed. I'm not sure I realized that was what I was experiencing at the time. I did understand that it wasn't right, and because I liked it, assumed there was something wrong with me. I didn't know how to change my behavior or if I even wanted to. I had no idea my heart was longing for a relationship with a Savior that would fill the void I felt. It was the beginning of my journey to find my value and significance in all the wrong ways and places. I always felt I was meant for something special in life. I would dream of changing the world and helping people. Looking back, I realize I didn't have a sense of my true identity. I felt insecure and afraid and just wanted to be seen and accepted. It would be years before I met the Holy Spirit. I knew I loved Jesus but never felt worthy and knew I would always fall short of His expectations.

I spent a lot of my time attending self-help seminars and feeling better for a while, but it never lasted. I was invited to church by a waitress at a local cafe. The church was literally down the street from where I grew up. I had never attended the church but had driven past it a thousand times. It was in that church that my pastors taught me about the love and grace of Jesus. They loved me unconditionally and with overwhelming grace. They taught me I could trust in the love and grace of Jesus. It was then that I knew and could trust in a personal relationship with a God who was real and my friend.

Along with my personal journey, I have had the opportunity to help and counsel many individuals, couples, and families in their journey towards emotional well-being. The theme that runs true for everyone is this—how do I avoid pain, disappointment, rejection, and abandonment? Sadly, the answer is we don't! Just because we may not consciously address our issues does not mean we are not affected by them. They tend to be hindrances and to keep us stuck.

Trying to avoid pain leads to putting up walls and not allowing anyone too close. When we love, it always means we are risking the pain of loss and grief. Disappointment is a human reality. There is always evidence to substantiate that people will disappoint you and/ or you will disappoint them. Having this information can create the need to make up stories about how people can't be trusted. Rejection and abandonment are overwhelmingly tied to our identity and what we believe to be true about ourselves. We put on masks so that when we are rejected or abandoned, we can tell ourselves they didn't really know us anyway. I realize these issues are more complex and could be an entire book all on their own. Instead, I would like to focus on how to move forward toward emotional well-being.

I believe one of the first practical steps for spiritual wholeness starts with being willing to give up control and let the Lord guide your healing. A mentor said to me recently, "Your belief that there is something wrong with you that you need to fix is your way of trying to control God." It took me some time to evaluate the statement. Deciding what we need to change on our own is the definition of operating out of our own strength and not relying on Him. It is a way of staying focused on me instead of Him and who He says I am. My conclusion is that trusting God with my life and surrendering to Him is much more frightening than deciding what I think needs to be fixed. It also takes away my excuse to stay small and not answer His call on my life. Staying small can be not volunteering to lead at my church, not hosting a Bible study, or not applying for a promotion at work. After all, if I still need to be fixed, it disqualifies me from moving forward.

A second practical step for spiritual wholeness is to accept that when we move forward, we will experience resistance. Resistance isn't always the devil. It can be lies or unhealthy mindsets that we learned based on our past. The teacher who told you that you will never make it in life or you're just not smart enough. A sibling who teased you and made you feel insecure and self-conscious. The patterns and cycles that are developed as a result of our life experiences. Even the patterns that are self-destructive are still what we know and understand. Change means taking risks and being vulnerable. It can mean having that difficult conversation with a friend or co-worker, asking for help and not isolating, being intentional and taking our thoughts and beliefs captive on a daily basis, or re-evaluating and believing that what God says about us is the truth.

> The truth is we are whole, healed, and have everything we need in this moment in Jesus.

A third practical step for spiritual wholeness is to recognize the resistance and have a process in place to manage our relationship with our hearts and the Lord. This is a critical step to moving toward emotional well-being. It is learning to recognize the patterns and cycles in our lives when we are trying to control the Lord or when we are operating out of our own strength and understanding. It is the place where we learn tools and create a process that enables us to change no matter the circumstances. It brings us back to our heart and relationship with the Lord. It is the place we learn to listen to the Lord and ask Him what He would have us do.

Emotional wellbeing is attainable; it's a process of learning to trust the Lord and yourself. The truth is we are whole, healed, and have everything we need in this moment in Jesus. Any thoughts or beliefs we have that don't come into alignment with this truth are opportunities to grow. When we become aware of what those thoughts and beliefs are, we have the privilege of bringing them to Jesus. He will let us know what He wants us to do with the information. He may say, "I don't want you to change anything. I just wanted you to see how it affects you." He may say, "Let's work on that together." It is in His kindness toward us that He doesn't leave us where we are.

> It is in His kindness toward us that He doesn't leave us where we are.

Our responsibility is to have a process in place and realize that we are not in this alone. If you would like to learn new tools and build your own process for sustainable emotional health, I am here to help. I have over thirty years of experience helping individuals and families. In a session, we will explore any belief systems you have that are barriers to you moving forward.

CHAPTER TWENTY-FIVE

When To Pursue More Healing

After a healing encounter, the most common question my clients ask me is, "When should I have another session?" Usually, I will let them know that the goal is not to engage in continual sessions with me. There is a time and a place to receive help and guidance from others, but all my resources, including an Identity Coaching session, are designed to equip you to be able to process on your own and live a lifestyle of freedom. Sometimes we can process with God on our own, and sometimes we need help. In this chapter we will explore how to know when we need help to pursue more healing.

By this time, you hopefully have accepted your need for ongoing healing. We are all in a process of discovering our true identity. As we have already looked at, healing is a manifested revelation of truth through spiritual discernment. The truth of who we are in Christ is already true, we just do not fully know, believe, or live out that truth. If our thoughts, attitudes, behaviors, and lives do not represent Jesus, it is because we are believing lies and self-protecting in our own effort. What we are being "healed" of are the lies and self-protections. Acknowledging our need for healing is not a sign of weakness, it is a sign of courage and honesty.

One way we could look at our healing journey is just to look at it in terms of discipleship. Our healing journey is really a discipleship journey. We follow Jesus and are disciples by faith, not by knowledge. That is why we must go beyond our intellect and knowledge to get to our beliefs. Repentance and obedience are from the heart. As the Word tells us in Ephesians 4:13, we are on a continual journey until we attain to the unity of the faith and knowledge of Jesus, to the full measure of maturity and stature of Christ. I am not sure about you, but I can guarantee you that I have not attained that maturity yet. Until I do, I will continue to pursue healing.

Acknowledging our need for healing is not a sign of weakness, it is a sign of courage and honesty.

Maybe when we look exactly like Jesus in every aspect of our lives, we can consider our healing journey complete. If we don't represent Jesus completely, and there seems to be a need for healing, the question is, "When do we pursue more healing?" On any journey, we are not always actively engaged in every aspect of the journey. There are seasons of focus as we are moving forward. Another way we can think about our healing journey could be to imagine a road trip. The focus of this journey is the pursuit of the kingdom of God first in everything we do. On this road trip, freedom, peace, and joy is where we are going. As we are driving, we have our favorite music playing, we are enjoying the journey and looking forward to our destination.

While on our trip, maybe we encounter some disruptions like road construction, or a traffic jam, or maybe we have to swerve to avoid an accident, or we even hit some potholes. On this trip, we will have trouble. We will run into minor inconveniences. We may have some unhealthy feelings or attitudes that rise up during this time. Maybe a moment of fear, shame, or guilt happens. That is OK, it happens. There is no need to pull over and check for problems. We do not need to do maintenance for every bump we hit or disturbance we have. The difference would be, if instead of a minor bump in the road, you start having a constant thump, thump, thump of fear, shame, or guilt. You could also have smoke coming from under the hood, or one or more of the gauges on your dashboard indicating a problem. That would be the time to pull over and find out what the issue is before it causes more problems.

Once you have experienced a pit stop and have resolved the issue that was causing the thump, smoke, or indicator reading, let yourself enjoy the ride for a while. There is no need to look for issues that may be there. If there is no evidence of a problem, I do not recommend looking for one. Jesus has set us free so that we can enjoy our freedom, not so that we can become yoked to the slavery of having to constantly look for issues to be resolved. We are not slaves to our issues. We are slaves to righteousness. Allow yourself to be free and enjoy your journey of peace.

While you are maturing and living your life, becoming more aware, establishing new boundaries, and communicating your needs, you will eventually find new areas of opportunity for growth. As we already talked about, we have intellectual, emotional, spiritual, physical, and relational boundaries that we are managing. Self-protections are not the same as boundaries. The difference between a wall of self-protection and a boundary is that boundaries still allow others to see you, experience you, and have the choice to honor you. They are flexible and movable based on your needs. A wall is immovable, impenetrable, impersonal, and gives people no choice. As you have choices and allow others to have choices, you will discover the health of the relationship.

If you can be present in your life and experience freedom, peace, and joy—do it! Use the healthy tools you have learned to live, thrive, and grow. If you are experiencing ongoing fear, shame, or guilt, find out why. Often, people repeatedly tell their stories of past trauma. This would be an example of the thump, thump, thump we looked at earlier. If you find yourself retelling old stories of your past trauma, here is a simple gauge to help you. If you have shared the story more than seven times (Joshua 6) and it is not a testimony, it is time to pursue healing. This is an extremely easy tool to use to let yourself know whether you are getting stuck in a loop of reliving the unresolved trauma, or if you are healed of it.

All of us need affirmation and understanding in our journey of healing. There is a legitimate need to share our stories. Unfortunately, the continual retelling of past trauma keeps us in a loop of reexperiencing the hurt and pain of that trauma. This is destructive to our emotional, mental, physical, and spiritual health. You do not have to continue doing this to yourself. Freedom in Christ is available. If you are stuck in one of these loops, and you can't process it yourself, seek help. If you want help working through it yourself, get my book *Identity Restoration*. If you would like someone to help you work through it, consider an Identity Coaching session.

There is not something wrong with you if you need to pursue more healing. Remember, all of us are on this healing journey together. You are not uniquely screwed up. You are uniquely created in Christ for good works that God prepared beforehand (Ephesians 2:10). You have permission to live free while experiencing freedom, peace, and joy. If things do not seem right, you also have permission to examine yourself to see whether you are believing lies and self-protecting.

CHAPTER TWENTY-SIX

The Importance of Discernment

Discernment is an important aspect of our maturity. Healthy discernment is not something that happens when we are triggered into an unresolved trauma. Often, I have found that people think they are discerning when they are just projecting a predetermined opinion on a situation based off of their own woundedness. Now that you have experienced a healing encounter, it should be easier for you to discern rather than believing lies, self-protecting, and projecting.

To start, let's look at some Scriptures that talk about discernment.

> Do not be conformed to this world, but be transformed by the renewal of your mind, that by testing you may discern what is the will of God, what is good and acceptable and perfect.
> – Romans 12:2

For the fruit of light is found in all that is good and right and true, and try to discern what is pleasing to the Lord.
– Ephesians 5:9-10

The word used in these two Scriptures for discern is Strong's G1381, dokimazō. It means: To test, approve, allow, discern, examine, prove, try.

The natural person does not accept the things of the Spirit of God, for they are folly to him, and he is not able to understand them because they are spiritually discerned.
– 1 Corinthians 2:14

The word used in this Scripture for discerned is Strong's G350, anakrinō. It means: To properly scrutinize, investigate, interrogate, determine, question, discern, examine, judge, search.

And it is my prayer that your love may abound more and more, with knowledge and all discernment.
– Philippians 1:9

The word used in this Scripture for discernment is Strong's G144, aisthēsis. It means: Perception, discernment, judgment.

But solid food is for the mature, for those who have their powers of discernment trained by constant practice to distinguish good from evil.
– Hebrews 5:14

The word used in this Scripture for discernment is Strong's G1253, diakrisis. It means: Judicial estimation, discern, disputation (debate).

Each of these words together express discernment and discerning as testing, approving, allowing, examining, proving, trying, properly scrutinizing, investigating, interrogating, determining, questioning, judging, searching, perceiving, judicially estimating, and debating. This is so much more than just feeling something. The most common mistake people make regarding discernment is they will just accept what they are feeling as a fact of what they think they are discerning.

When we are triggered, we often confuse the feelings we have, based on the lie we are triggered into, as discernment. Our feelings are a necessary aspect of discernment, but relying on our feelings for discernment is misleading and destructive. We need to allow ourselves to feel our emotions, examine those emotions, scrutinize them, determine why we are feeling them, and perceive what is truly happening. We cannot just rely on a gut feeling as a final answer. I am not saying we need to discount or deny our feelings. I am saying we need to allow, test, discern, examine, properly scrutinize, investigate, determine, question, judge, and search out our feelings. This will allow us to know the good, perfect, and acceptable will of God, to accept the things of the Spirit of God, to find what is good, right, true, and pleasing to the Lord, to abound in knowledge, and to distinguish good from evil.

> Discernment requires emotional awareness and clarity of thought.

As we looked at in the I Think – I Feel chapter, understanding the difference between our thoughts and feelings is critical in the discerning process. Discernment requires emotional awareness and clarity of thought. If we are triggered by a lie, and are reacting out of unresolved trauma, we will not have the ability to discern properly. This is what causes us to project our predetermined opinion on situations.

What you think and feel about yourself directly affects your discernment. That is why healing and identity are so important. Now that you have experienced some level of healing and you can believe who you are based in Scriptural truth, you can discern from your true identity in ways you could not before. This will begin to change how you perceive people and situations, especially if you were previously codependently finding your identity in other situations, people, or events. If you were finding your identity in other things, you were not able to properly discern and make good choices. Now that you can be "you," you can discern properly, and make healthy choices.

This will be a new experience for some and will sometimes include emotional swings now that you can see clearly. It is OK. Having awareness of the functional dysfunction, the old tools, and the pendulum swings are all part of the maturity process and will help you discern more effectively. Don't expect to be an expert right away. Take your time and let yourself practice discernment. Test it, examine it, scrutinize it, question it, investigate it, and perceive. Check and see how your discernment lines up with the truth of the Word.

Discernment is a natural aspect of your identity in Christ.

Remember, Holy Spirit is revealing all truth to us. Even the healing you experienced was a revelation of truth through spiritual discernment. Discernment is a natural aspect of your identity in Christ. Allow yourself to have emotions. Consider the thoughts you have. Practice capturing your thoughts, bring them into the light, reconsider them, and believe the truth. When you can properly discern, you will understand the will of God, accept the truth from Holy Spirit, experience the fruit of being pleasing to God, allow your love to abound in knowledge, and be able to distinguish good from evil. This will help you mature into yourself as a child of God. You can do this. Be free and enjoy your peace.

CHAPTER TWENTY-SEVEN

Personal Responsibility

The term personal responsibility can potentially stir up excitement and hope, or it can stir up fear and shame. Think about what it would be like if you could take personal responsibility for everything in your life and thrive in freedom, peace, and joy.

What I mean by personal responsibility is intentionally taking ownership of our thoughts, emotions, choices, decisions, behaviors, relationships, attitudes, needs, and direction in life. I believe that personal responsibility is one of the greatest keys to freedom. Without it, we will struggle to have our basic needs met and to fully experience our righteousness, peace, and joy.

> For the kingdom of God is not a matter of eating and drinking but of righteousness and peace and joy in the Holy Spirit.
> – Romans 14:17

When sin entered the world through the lies of the enemy, fear, shame, and guilt began stealing our purpose, killing our security, and destroying our relationships. Purpose, security, and relationship are basic needs that are foundational in the kingdom. Let's separately look at how each of these are affected by personal responsibility.

Security

The core of our security is our peace in the Holy Spirit. This peace is what will define the authority that we walk in as followers of Christ. When we can take personal responsibility for our peace in the Lord, we will have assurance in our security, contentment, and authority. This assurance will affect our ability to feel safe, to trust, and to rest in the truth of who we are in Christ. When we can trust and rest in the truth, patience and humility will flourish in our lives as we courageously walk in the victory of our faith.

Peace is a natural aspect of our identity in Christ. As I have explained in my book *Identity Restoration*, the enemy is trying to kill our authority by getting us to believe his lies. When we believe a lie about an aspect of our identity that is intended to manifest peace, we will manifest fear. This fear, unchecked, will eventually bring us to a place of powerlessness where we are tricked into thinking there is nothing we can do to experience peace. When we are powerless to accept personal responsibility for our own peace, we will attempt to control the circumstances, environments, relationships, and people in our lives to manage our peace and security. Control is at best a lack of personal responsibility, and at worst a refusal to be responsible for our own peace and security.

Now that you have experienced some level of healing, anywhere in your life that you were operating in fear and control, you can now take personal responsibility for your own peace and begin to trust God. What I mean by taking responsibility for our peace and security is to accept that our peace is a manifestation of our faith. What we think and believe will determine how we feel and whether we will experience peace or fear. Peace is a manifestation of believing the truth of who God is and who we are in Christ. When we believe it, we will feel it. You have the authority to believe the truth of who you are in Christ and to live in peace.

Purpose

The core of our purpose is joy in the Holy Spirit. This joy is what will determine the expression of our identity in Christ. When we can take personal responsibility for our joy in the Lord, we will have the affirmation of our purpose, approval, and identity. This affirmation will affect our ability to feel accepted, to hope, and to delight in the truth of who we are in Christ. When we can hope and delight in the truth, gratitude and determination will flourish in our lives as we optimistically walk in the fulfillment of our faith.

Joy is a natural aspect of our identity in Christ. The enemy is trying to steal our identity by getting us to believe his lies. When we believe a lie about an aspect of our identity that is intended to manifest joy, we will manifest shame. This shame, unchecked, will eventually bring us to a place of helplessness where we are tricked into thinking there is no hope for joy. When we are hopeless and cannot take personal responsibility for our own joy, we will attempt to find joy and purpose in our status, our finances, our career, or any number of false identities.

Now that you have experienced some level of healing, anywhere in your life that you were stuck in shame and false identities, you can now take personal responsibility for your own joy, purpose, and hope in the Lord. What I mean by taking responsibility for our joy and purpose is to accept that our joy is a manifestation of our faith. What we think and believe about ourselves, and God, will determine whether we will experience joy or shame. God purposely created you with clarity, and you have permission to live in joy.

Relationship

The core of our relationships is our righteousness and freedom in the Holy Spirit. This freedom is what will define our relationships in Christ. When we can take personal responsibility for our freedom, we will have confidence in our relationships and community. This confidence will affect our ability to feel loved, respected, and connected. When we feel loved and respected in our relationships, we will have compassion, empathy, and generosity flourishing in our lives as we walk in the kindness and harmony of our faith.

> When we can accept personal responsibility for our own freedom, peace, and joy, we will experience security and purpose in our lives and relationships.

Freedom is a natural aspect of our identity in Christ. The enemy is trying to destroy our community by getting us to believe his lies. When we believe a lie about an aspect of our identity that is intended to manifest freedom, we will manifest guilt. This guilt, unchecked, will eventually bring us to a place of loneliness where we are tricked into thinking we are being punished and there is no way to be free. This lonely punishment will keep us from taking personal responsibility for our own freedom, and we will isolate ourselves and blame others for it.

Now that you have experienced some level of healing, anywhere in your life that you were alone in guilt and blame, you can now take personal responsibility for your own freedom and experience your righteous relationship with God. What I mean by taking responsibility for our freedom and relationships is to accept that our freedom is a manifestation of our faith. What we think and believe about ourselves, God, and others will determine whether we will experience guilt or freedom. You are righteous in Christ; you belong to Him and you can live free.

When we can accept personal responsibility for our own freedom, peace, and joy, we will experience security and purpose in our lives and relationships. When we do not, this will lead us into unhealthy, codependent relationships with people, circumstances, and things. These unhealthy relationships will keep us hiding in fear, covering ourselves in shame, and blaming others in guilt.

Personal responsibility is a blessing, not a burden.

This personal responsibility all starts with taking ownership of our own thoughts and emotions. When we can accept that our emotions are a result of our thoughts and beliefs, we can begin to experience joy in our purpose, security in our peace, and freedom in our relationships.

Personal responsibility is a blessing, not a burden. As we take ownership of our own thoughts and emotions, we can steward our needs in a healthy way. You were created with needs, and you have permission to have your needs met in freedom, peace, and joy.

CHAPTER TWENTY-EIGHT

Grateful Celebration

The concept of gratitude and celebration was not always normal for me. I grew up in a family culture of negativity, complaining, and mental and emotional abuse. That dysfunctional culture was a foundational influence on my thinking and processing. This helped develop my addiction to negativity and rejection. It took me years of healing and many encounters with the Lord to break this cycle. It still is not always easy for me to celebrate and be grateful. I must intentionally focus on it.

Along with the cultural and generational influences that each one of us must conquer and rise above, there are some biological issues we have to overcome as well. There is something called negativity bias that all of us must deal with. Some psychological research shows that our brains react more strongly to negative stimuli, and we need at least a five-to-one ratio of positivity to negativity just to have an equilibrium.

This negativity bias can cause you to remember traumatic experiences more often than good experiences, ruminate on negative details, focus on criticism, and more easily believe lies about yourself, your situation, and others. This can be destructive to your self-image, your purpose, and your relationships. Just think about that for a moment. Simply understanding and taking authority over this one biological hurdle can dramatically change your life.

> You can transition into a lifestyle of gratitude and celebration that will increase your freedom, peace, and joy.

This may or may not be an issue for you. You may have grown up in a healthier environment where you were trained to think more positively and be grateful. Praise God if that is you! If that is not you, don't worry; freedom is available. Especially now that you have experienced some level of healing, the ability to be grateful and think more positively will be more natural. As I mentioned, I was addicted to negativity, and would fixate on criticism, rejection, and regret. It was an extreme and miserable issue for me. I am no longer stuck there! If I can be free, you can be free. You can transition into a lifestyle of gratitude and celebration that will increase your freedom, peace, and joy.

There are many coaching clients who I have worked with who were trained to deny their thoughts and pretend and perform an image of positivity. That is not what I am talking about. We still need to capture every thought and bring it into the obedience of Christ. We must acknowledge and consider our negative thoughts so we can reconsider and believe the good news. The positive reality of Jesus

Christ is good news. Changing your thinking patterns may take practice and training, but it is possible, and it is worth it.

We can start with the simple celebration that you have made it this far in the maturing into yourself process. Just the fact that you have pressed in this far with this book and this process is evidence of maturity. I am so grateful that you are still reading, listening, learning, and hopefully being blessed. I never stop being amazed that what I have learned through my trauma and my healing brings healing to others. That is something I can easily celebrate and be grateful for, even though there are negative thoughts that still creep in that I need to capture and bring into the light.

As we looked at in the Building Faith chapter, one of the ways to build faith is to remember and celebrate what God has done. Let's review some of the growth we have experienced so far and celebrate it. We have become aware of, and have taken personal responsibility for, our emotional and mental health. We can be present, discern, establish boundaries, communicate our needs, and adjust our dysfunctional relationships. We know ourselves better, can now accept ourselves, love ourselves, nurture ourselves, and better care for our needs. We can dream, believe in ourselves, and pursue healing freely. We are more free. You are more free!

As we looked at in chapter twenty-one, the Lord often instructed His followers to build memorials, have feasts, and establish traditions of celebration. We can find these patterns of celebration in the Old and New Testament. I hope these Scriptures are an inspiration to you.

> Then Samuel took a stone and set it up between Mizpah and Shen and called its name Ebenezer; for he said, "Till now the LORD has helped us."
> – 1 Samuel 7:12

This verse in 1 Samuel came to mind and reminded me of the hymn, "Come Though Fount." If you can, I recommend taking some time and letting yourself meditate on the presence of God and how He has helped you, while listening to this hymn. It is a beautiful and moving experience.

> And bring the fattened calf and kill it, and let us eat and celebrate. For this my son was dead, and is alive again; he was lost, and is found.' And they began to celebrate.
> – Luke 15:23-24

We can now come to God in confidence, in sincerity, and in the truth of who we are in Christ.

This verse in Luke reminded me of how the Father celebrates our return to Him. If you can, I recommend taking some time and celebrating with the Lord that you once were dead, but now you are alive in Him. You were lost, but now you are found. Another great experience could be meditating on the presence of God and celebrating with Him while listening to the hymn, "Amazing Grace."

> Let us therefore celebrate the festival, not with the old leaven, the leaven of malice and evil, but with the unleavened bread of sincerity and truth.
> – 1 Corinthians 5:8

This verse in 1 Corinthians reminded me of another verse:

For whenever our heart condemns us, God is greater than our

heart, and He knows everything. Beloved, if our heart does not condemn us, we have confidence before God.
– 1 John 3:20-21

We no longer need to come to God in condemnation. Even if our hearts do condemn us, God is greater. We can now come to God in confidence, in sincerity, and in the truth of who we are in Christ. These verses remind me of my all-time favorite hymn, "How Great Thou Art." If you can, I recommend taking the time to come confidently to the Lord in praise, while listening to this hymn, and let your soul sing out in celebration for what God has done for you.

There are many memorial stones we can look back on and celebrate. If you are willing, take a moment and look back on your journey of healing and maturing. Yes, I know it probably has been at least a little messy, but freedom is always better. It would be a great exercise for you to pause here and write this out so you can celebrate the memorial stones of accomplishments through your healing and maturing journey. If you do experience negative thoughts during this exercise, apply the five-to-one ratio and see how it goes for you. For each negative thought, find at least five things to celebrate and be grateful for. This ratio may be a little different for each one of us. I have seen the negative bias explained as four to seven times more powerful than positivity in our brains. Five is not a magic number. Practice and see what works for you.

Of course, positive thoughts do not necessarily change your situation. Transitioning your thinking to be more thankful and grateful can help give you the hope to be able to make a change, but there is more to it than that.

Along with the negativity bias we all have, some of us will have even more challenges we need to work through. I personally have to manage this process while dealing with my mood disorder. It is much easier for me to think positively when I am in a neutral or hypomanic state. When I am in a depressive state, I must work much harder at this process. You may be struggling with a mental or emotional disorder yourself that adds extra challenges. It is OK, you can do this. You can be free and enjoy your peace.

> Finally, brothers, whatever is true, whatever is honorable, whatever is just, whatever is pure, whatever is lovely, whatever is commendable, if there is any excellence, if there is anything worthy of praise, think about these things. What you have learned and received and heard and seen in me—practice these things, and the God of peace will be with you.
> – Philippians 4:8-9

Remember, this Scripture is more than a command. It is written on your heart and already fulfilled in you by the work of Jesus. This is an aspect of your identity in Christ.

CHAPTER TWENTY-NINE

What Now?

Sometimes I ponder and think about odd things. One of the things I have been thinking about and observing recently is how much we are imagining our lives instead of being present and experiencing our lives. Now that you have experienced some level of healing, you can be present and experience life instead of imagining it.

If we think about the question, "What now?" or "What do I do now?" I think the answer may be to be present and experience life. I realize this is a vague statement. There are aspects to this we need to look at, but before we do, let's look back and see how far you have come. Hopefully, you were able to engage in the exercise from the Grateful Celebration chapter and look back on your journey to celebrate your memorial stones of maturity. You are now more aware of yourself and your relationships, retooled for success, establishing healthier boundaries for yourself, letting yourself think your thoughts and feel your feelings, taking responsibility for your thoughts and feelings, getting to know yourself better, holistically taking care of yourself, growing in your faith, believing in yourself, dreaming again, establishing healthier life patterns, discerning truth, and celebrating your success. If all went well during this process, you are experiencing life a little differently than you did before your healing encounter. You are different. You think differently, see differently, and can discern truth more effectively. This is a great place to be. Now that you are here, what do you do?

The real answer to that question never changes for me. In every step of our process, we seek first the kingdom of God and His righteousness. Each practical step may look different, but the foundation of each of them always needs to be based in seeking the kingdom of God.

In chapter ten of my book *Identity Restoration*, I break out this concept.

> But seek first the kingdom of God and His righteousness, and all these things will be added to you.
> – Matthew 6:33

> For the kingdom of God is not a matter of eating and drinking but of righteousness and peace and joy in the Holy Spirit.
> – Romans 14:17

The Greek word used in Matthew 6:33 for seek is zèteò (Strong's G2212). It means: To seek (literally or figuratively), worship God, be about, go about, desire, endeavor, enquire for, require, seek after, seek for.

The Greek word used in Matthew 6:33 for first is proton (Strong's G4412). It means: Firstly (in time, place, order, or importance), before, at the beginning, chiefly, first, first of all.

An expression of those two Scriptures including the fullness of those definitions could be:

Worship God by being about, going about, desiring, endeavoring for, enquiring for, requiring, and seeking His kingdom of righteousness, peace, and joy first, at the beginning, in the first order of importance, before anything else, and all these things will be added to you.

It is good to remember that we are on a journey of pursuing righteousness, peace, and joy, not a journey of pursuing unresolved trauma to get healed from. Jesus set us free so we could be free. He did not set us free to submit to a yoke of slavery (Galatians 5:1). We are slaves to righteousness, not fear, shame, and guilt.

You are free to live free.

Hopefully, in the areas where you were stuck and had a fixed mindset, you are now freer in your thinking and can have a growth mindset. You can continue to grow, to know God better, and to know yourself more clearly. You are free to live free.

Being stuck in a loop of finding and resolving trauma is not what I would call freedom. The pursuit of healing is the pursuit of the kingdom of God. We don't need to focus on or worry about past traumas that have caused current lies. There is a delicate balance of acknowledging the truth of who we are, along with the reality that we do not fully believe that truth and are in a healing process. Remember, healing is just a manifested revelation of truth through spiritual discernment. The truth is already true, we just don't always believe it. We don't want a victim mindset of the constant need for healing, and we don't want a denial mindset of thinking we have already resolved all our issues. We need to accept that we are on a journey of discovery.

> He who descended is the one who also ascended far above all the heavens, that He might fill all things. And He gave the apostles, the prophets, the evangelists, the shepherds and teachers, to equip the saints for the work of ministry, for building up the body of Christ, until we all attain to the unity of the faith and of the knowledge of the Son of God, to mature manhood, to the measure of the stature of the fullness of Christ, so that we may no longer be children, tossed to and fro by the waves and carried about by every wind of doctrine, by human cunning, by craftiness in deceitful schemes.
> – Ephesians 4:10-14

When we all reach the unity of the faith and the maturity of the full measure of the stature of Christ, we can say we are done with this healing journey. Until then, we need to repent and believe the good news, continue to follow Jesus into life, pursue the kingdom of God, and check to see if we are in the faith when behaviors, attitudes, actions, or mindsets arise that do not look like Jesus.

You have permission to live, to live free, and to live abundantly.

In Deuteronomy, the Word tells us that the Lord gave us choices. We can choose life or death, blessing or curses. Therefore, choose life and blessing so that you may live a blessed life.

As you are seeking the kingdom of God first, these are some things you can do now. All the desires of your new clean heart that have been stirred—pursue them! All the hopes that have been renewed—pursue them! All the dreams that have been rebirthed—pursue them! You have permission to live, to live free, and to live abundantly. Explore your creativity that may have been set free, learn the things you have been wanting to learn, and try the things you have been wanting to try. It is never too late to live free.

To be able to pursue these things, we need to be present and experience real life. The unresolved trauma and lies in our lives cause us to trigger off into our imagination of fear, shame, and guilt in our past or future, instead of being present. As I mentioned in the beginning of this chapter, so much of our lives are stolen by this imagination. Therefore it is incredibly important to intentionally stay present, choose reality, and connect with God.

> ...for behold, the kingdom of God is in the midst of you.
> – Luke 17:21

The kingdom of God, of righteousness, peace, and joy in the Holy Spirit, is in our midst. It is not in our triggered imaginations of fear, shame, or guilt. That would be the kingdom of the world in our own effort. If we are to pursue the kingdom of God first, we need to acknowledge when we are triggered into the kingdom of the world, and no longer settle for it.

You have permission to try, to make mistakes, and to fail. None of these affect your identity. Trust your heart, check your thoughts, and connect with God. He is faithful and wants to fulfill the desires of your heart. Remember from the Self-Nurture chapter, discipleship is following Jesus into life. Living involves growth. You have permission to grow, to mature, and to be more like Christ. You can do this. I am proud of you for being this far on your journey. You are so much more amazing than you even know. God created you in His image to fulfill a purpose. In Christ, you can be secure in your purpose and valuable and free in your relationships.

Thank you for letting me
be a part of your
healing journey.

I pray that you may
live your life free
and healed in all
the fullness of your
Identity in Christ!

Ray

RECOMMENDATIONS

For help finding your identity, resolving any fear, shame, or guilt, and living in freedom, peace, and joy:

Individual Coaching Sessions:
www.faithbygrace.org/identity-coaching

Online course:
equip.identityrestoration.net

For help finding a local counselor:
www.psychologytoday.com

For help finding an online counselor:
www.betterhelp.com
try.talkspace.com

RESOURCES

Ray's Resources:

Identity Restoration

If you desire a lifestyle of freedom, peace, and joy - this is the book for you! It is a culmination of over 20 years of in-depth study and real-world experience, that has been refined into a lifestyle of freedom that you can easily implement. You will be equipped with practical and sustainable tools to help you go from a false normal of fear, shame, or guilt into a kingdom lifestyle of freedom, peace, and joy, in any situation or circumstance. Be equipped and empowered to know who you are, believe who you are, and live out the fullness of that truth in the power of the Holy Spirit. Freedom is available!

www.faithbygrace.org/identity-restoration

Who Do You Think You Are? Bible Study - Volume One

This is one of the most comprehensive resources available to discover your identity in Christ, and to be transformed into that truth. You will have the opportunity to read through hundreds of Scriptures, in context, and get revelation of over 250 different aspects of your identity in Christ. It focuses on your redeemed, alive, righteous, fruitful, pure, and accepted identity in Christ.

www.faithbygrace.org/who-do-you-think-you-are_bible-study

Who Do You Think You Are? Devotional - Volume One

This 21-Day Devotional will give you the chance to daily review the truth of who God says you are, process your thoughts and beliefs, and help you align with His truth. You will receive revelation about your redeemed, alive, righteous, fruitful, pure, and accepted identity in Christ as you are walked through a process to develop statements of faith, from the Scriptures, that you believe and can declare over yourself. As you experience this devotional, you will be able to dream about how your life can look as you believe the truth of your identity in Christ and work out practical steps you can take to live the fullness of your life. This devotional will transform your thinking and your understanding of who you are in Christ.

www.faithbygrace.org/Who-do-you-think-you-are_devotional

Finding A New Normal

Grieving isn't easy. In fact, it's one of the hardest things we will ever do. This is an invitation and a guide to help you be real in your grief, honest about your needs, and equipped to process the trauma of your loss. This book was written in the midst of my own grief, following the loss of our home in the Northern California Carr fire of 2018. No matter where you are in your grieving process, Finding A New Normal will meet you there.

www.faithbygrace.org/finding-a-new-normal1

Other Resources:

Your Dream Journal – Colleen De Silva

In *Your Dream Journal*, Colleen De Silva simplifies dream interpretation through practical tips, easy-to-follow steps, definitions to key images, and an in-depth dream sample. Each section sets you up for a fun and stress-free experience when journaling and interpreting your own dreams, while emphasizing the importance of inviting the Holy Spirit into your process. God loves to speak to us in the night while our bodies rest and our spirits are awake. *Your Dream Journal* will set you on an adventure with Father God, Jesus, and Holy Spirit as you discover strategies, dreams, giftings, and callings through stewarding your dreams!

Available at Amazon.com, Fall 2022

Feeling Good – David D. Burns, M.D.

The good news is that anxiety, guilt, pessimism, procrastination, low self-esteem, and other "black holes" of depression can be cured without drugs. In *Feeling Good*, eminent psychiatrist, David D. Burns, M.D., outlines the remarkable, scientifically proven techniques that will immediately lift your spirits and help you develop a positive outlook on life. Now, in this updated edition, Dr. Burns adds an All-New Consumer's Guide To Anti-depressant Drugs as well as a new introduction to help answer your questions about the many options available for treating depression.

Available at Amazon.com

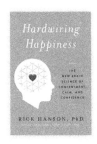

Hardwiring Happiness - Rick Hanson Ph.D.

Hardwiring Happiness lays out a simple method that uses the hidden power of everyday experiences to build new neural structures full of happiness, love, confidence, and peace. You'll learn to see through the lies your brain tells you. Dr. Hanson's four steps build strengths into your brain to make contentment and a powerful sense of resilience the new normal. In just minutes a day, you can transform your brain into a refuge and power center of calm and happiness.

Available at Amazon.com